Joe Pauker

# *GET LOST!*

## The Cool Guide to Amsterdam

*Thai* ✗✗✗

*Noethern lights* ✗✗

*Bubblegum* ✗

*Super Shiva* ✗✗✗✗✗

*White Widow* ✗✗✗

*Power Jack* ✗✗✗

*Power Plant* ✗✗

*BIO* ✗✗

## Get Lost Publishing

## May 1999

British Library in Publication Data. A catalogue record for this book is available from the British Library.

© Get Lost Publishing, May 1999

ISBN: 90-802561-0-2

**For all their help, advice, information, and support, many thanks to...**
Aaron, American Book Center, Amsterdam Call Girls, Anthony, Barbara, Candy, Christian & Ann, Claudia, Clyde, Curt & Nancy, Dave, Global Chillage, The Headshop, Hemp Hotel, Klaus, Kokopelli, Krul, Mack, Michel, Mom, Monica, Mor & Fred, Natascha, Pip, Pop, Richard & Elard, Rick, Roland, Rosa & Art, Sagarmatha Seeds, Sensi Seed Bank, Steve B, Steve D, Susan, Uln & Charlie, Victor & Catarina... and most of all, Lisa.

Editing and research assistance by **Lisa Kristensen**

Cover design by **Ellen Pauker**

Photos by **Joe Pauker**

**Printed in Amsterdam with vegetable-based inks
on 100% post-consumer-waste recycled paper.**

QUESTION
AUTHORITY

# INTRODUCTION

Congratulations! You're in the most happening city in Europe and you've got a copy of *Get Lost!* Inside, you'll find the things that I look for when I visit a new city: cool, underground places that often aren't found in other guides, plus all the practical information I need to find my way around easily and quickly. I wrote the first edition of *The Cool Guide* seven years ago during a period when I didn't have a TV. I borrowed a friend's computer, and spent a week typing up my hand-written manuscript. When I returned the computer (this is a true story), my friend plugged it in and it blew up! I distributed that edition using only my bicycle and both of us (me and bike) were very happy when it sold out.

This new edition has been completely revised and updated. And it continues to be an independent, DIY project. We've sold a few ads to help us cover the costs of printing and paper, but nobody pays to be included in *Get Lost!*

While we were unable to get any hemp paper for this edition, we're happy to be using vegetable-based inks for the first time. The book is printed on 100% post-consumer-waste recycled paper. It also now has a stitched binding.

I've tried to be very accurate with regard to prices, opening times, etc, but I'm just a goof, and things change. I love getting mail, so feel free to write if you have any suggestions, complaints, or spare change.

Be sure to check the Get Lost Publishing home page on the Internet for updates on the places and info included in *The Cool Guide*.

Thanks for buying this edition of *Get Lost!* Have a great trip!

**Get Lost!**
Box 18521
1001 WB  Amsterdam
The Netherlands

**Home Page:**
*http://www.xs4all.nl/~getlost*

**Also Available:**
Get Lost! The Cool Guide to San Francisco
Get Lost! Der Coole Reiseführer - Amsterdam

# CONTENTS

# ABOUT THE AUTHOR

Joe Pauker was conceived in a test tube as part of an early CIA experiment. While still a child, he escaped from the military compound where he was being trained as a killing machine. Joe fled to the Caribbean where he fought with the Cubans at the Bay of Pigs. During the years that followed, he travelled the world: he marched with Martin Luther King in Birmingham, studied Shao Lin Kung Fu in Hong Kong, and was the youngest member of the Bay City Rollers. At 14 he ate a car. Later he gained brief notoriety when, after a drug- and alcohol-crazed year with the DiCaprio Posse, he streaked across the stage at the 1998 Oscar ceremonies. Joe Pauker now lives a quiet life in a monastery, where he writes guidebooks to cities that he's never visited.

# PLACES TO SLEEP

Although there's an abundance of luxury hotel rooms, there just aren't enough cheap hotel rooms for all the visitors to Amsterdam, especially in the summer. It can be a real drag finding a place to stay, and if you're in town for just a few days you don't want to waste time, so here are a few hints to help you out.

One of your best bets is to go with a "runner" (someone who has the shitty job of running back and forth between a hotel and the train station). These people work for small hotels or hostels, or for private homes and guest houses. A lot of the runners carry books with photos of the rooms so you can look at what you're getting before trekking over there. I've found some really great places this way. I've also seen some dives, but it doesn't cost to look.

In the summer a bed in a hostel runs anywhere from ƒ20-38 and a clean double room for less than ƒ120 is a good deal. In the winter (except around New Year's) it never hurts to bargain, and double rooms can be found for as little as ƒ70-80.

At the VVV tourist office (across the square in front of Central Station and to your left) they have a room finding service. They can book you a dorm bed at a cheaper price, but plain double rooms in high season start at ƒ100 (without bath) and of course these go fast. If you use the VVV you have to pay them a ƒ5 per person service charge and another ƒ5 per person as a deposit (which is later deducted from the price of the room). The people who work at the VVV are very nice and sometimes you can get a good deal, but in high season the line-ups are painfully long and slow.

The GWK bank at Central Station also has a room-finding service. There you pay a ƒ5 per person fee and the full amount of the hotel in advance. The fact that you can't see the place first is a drawback, but their "same-day" sell-off rates (on all grades of hotels) are sometimes a real bargain, especially off-season.

# HOSTELS

### Schiphol Airport

You know, I've slept in a lot of airports around the world, and Schiphol is definitely the best. They have comfortable couches in the departure lounges where you can actually lie down when you crash out. If you need to bathe there are showers in the Central Lounge (including soap and towel) for ƒ10. Or go to the Hotel Mercure (604-1339) near gate "F". They offer showers 24 hours a day in a private cabin (including soap, towel, and a hair dryer) for ƒ20, or a sauna and shower for ƒ25. As for breakfast, there are often free cheese samples on offer at the duty-free delicatessen. And upstairs, in the Panorama Lounge, a plate of stir-fried veggies costs just ƒ3,75. Of course, you wouldn't want to stay there for your whole trip, but if you have a morning flight and plan to be out dancing most of the night before you leave, it's a good way to save the cost of a night's lodging.

### Christian Youth Hostels (The Shelter, Eben Haezer)

Only ƒ20 for a dorm bed and breakfast makes these two hostels a great deal. But separate rooms for men and women, curfews, sing-alongs in the lounge, and a clean-cut

staff that's looking for converts should be enough to persuade you to spend a little more elsewhere. You'll have to find the addresses yourself.

**The Flying Pig** - *Nieuwendijk 100, 420-6822; Vossiusstraat 46-47, 400-4187*
*http://www.flyingpig.nl*

These hostels are popular with travellers. One, on Nieuwendijk (Flying Pig
Downtown), is very close to Central Station. The other (Flying Pig Palace) is by
Vondelpark. Rooms for one or two people cost ƒ90-110. At the Downtown, the rates
per person for shared rooms with 4 to 26 beds range from ƒ25 to ƒ39.50. The Palace
has shared rooms with 4 to 12 beds for ƒ25.50 to ƒ37.50 per person. A free, basic
breakfast is included. All rooms have toilets and showers. The guys who run these
places are travellers themselves, which explains such things as the free use of
kitchens, late night bars, and the absence of curfews. For hanging out, there's a
"happy room" in an old bank vault downstairs at Nieuwendijk, and both locations
have a TV lounge. Both sites are central, but the neighbourhood around Vondelpark
is much nicer. To reach the Palace from Central Station take tram 1, 2, 5, 11 or 20
to Leidseplein. Walk over the bridge to Vondelpark. The street runs along the left
side of the park. (Map areas D4, B8)

**Bob's Youth Palace** - *Nieuwezijds Voorburgwal 92, 623-0063*

You can usually find this hostel by looking for a bunch of people sitting on the front
steps smoking joints and strumming guitars. This is a pretty cool, clean place where
a lot of travellers stay. It's right in the centre of the city and ƒ25 gets you a dorm bed
and breakfast. They also have a women's dorm. Trams 1, 2, 5, 11, 13, 17 will take you
there, or you can walk from Central Station: it's not far. (Map area D4)

**International Budget Hotel** - *Leidsegracht 76, 624-2784*

I spent a few nights here once and liked it. The rooms, some with a canal view, are
plain and very clean, and if you're going to stay in a dorm it's nice that there are only
4 beds to a room. There's also a comfortable TV lounge, with tea, coffee and snacks
for sale. Everyone I met working there was really friendly - and that's important. A
bed in a 4 person dorm costs ƒ35-45 and there are a few double rooms from ƒ120.
The rates are cheaper off season. From Central Station take tram 1, 2, 5 or 20 to
Leidseplein and then it's a short walk. Also owned by the same folks is the Euphemia
Budget Hotel at Fokke Simonszstraat 1 (622-9045). They've done nice renovations
there and have some double rooms for ƒ85-125 (ƒ110-150 with shower and toilet)
and triple rooms for ƒ50-60 per person. (Map area C6)

**Arena** - *'s-Gravesandestraat 51, 694-7444*
*http://www.hotelarena.nl/enindex.html*

Years ago, this huge, old mansion was converted into a low-budget hostel because
the City wanted hippies to stop sleeping in Vondelpark. It turned into one of the
coolest hostels in town, in spite of being located a bit outside of the centre. Although
the atmosphere has become increasingly corporate over the years, the 435 beds and
the good facilities have insured that the Arena is still often a happening place.
There's a games room and computer area, a restaurant/bar (The Alfresco), and an
old concert hall that hosts weekly parties (see Music chapter). Depending on the season, a bed in a large dorm costs from ƒ20 to ƒ27.50. Smaller dorms for 4 to 8 people go for ƒ30 to ƒ37.50 per person. There are also women-only dorms in high season, as well as double and quad rooms (see Hotels, this chapter). All the rooms
have their own shower and toilet facilities. If you need them, blankets and sheets

cost an extra *f*5. Breakfast is not included. From Central Station take tram 9 to Mauritskade. Night bus 76 or 77. (Map area G8)

**The Bulldog** - *Oudezijds Voorburgwal 220, 620-3822*
*http://www.bulldog.nl/american/hotel.htm*

This hostel is located right in the Red Light District. The cheapest dorm beds go for *f*31.50 to *f*35, depending on the season. Smaller dorms with 8 beds and a shower and toilet in the room, run from *f*36.50 to *f*40 per person. Some of the dorms even have TVs. A coin that gets you 8 minutes worth of hot water in the shower is included in these prices. Extra coins cost *f*1.50. If you need them, sheets are *f*7.50; and, if you want it, breakfast is also *f*7.50. The rooms are very basic, but clean, and there's no curfew or lock-out. Single rooms go for *f*90-105; doubles for *f*110-120 (with shower and toilet - *f*120-130); triples for *f*165-175; and quads for *f*210-225. They're also talking about building a roof-top terrace, which would be great in the summer. (Map area D5)

**International Youth Hostels** - *Zandpad 5 (Vondelpark), 589-8996;*
*Kloveniersburgwal 97, 624-6832*
*http://www.njhc.org/vondelpark*

These are "official" youth hostels. The one in Vondelpark (a great location) has just been completely renovated and all their rooms are equipped with a toilet and shower. They offer dorm beds (*f*33.75-38), single rooms (*f*70-85), and twin rooms (*f*90-125). There are triple and quad rooms, too. Non-members pay a *f*5 surcharge. Sheets are included in the price, as is an all-you-can-eat breakfast. There are also restaurants, a bicycle rental service, and a tourist info centre. And I've been assured that, most of the time, groups of kids on field trips will be booked into a different building from the one housing independent travellers. From Central Station take tram 1,2 or 5 to Leidseplein. Walk to the Marriott Hotel, turn left. The hostel sign is just a block ahead of you. The other location is also nice: on a wide canal right in the centre of the city. There are only dorm rooms, however. Beds cost from *f*26.50 to *f*28.75 plus an additional *f*5 if you're a non-member. Note that there's a curfew here, but not at the Vondelpark hostel. (Map areas E6, B7)

# HOTELS

Here are a few places with clean, reasonably-priced rooms. In the summer you should really try to arrange your accommodation before leaving Central Station - through a runner, the VVV, the GWK, or by calling one of the hotels below.

The Netherlands Reservation Service (tel: 3170-419-5544 / fax: 3170-419-5519) will make free bookings at all grades of hotels throughout Holland. Just let them know what you want, when, and how much you're willing to pay. It's best to book with a credit card number. If you don't have one you can still make a reservation, but you'll have to check in early in the day. Open: mon-fri 8-20; sat 8-14.

Web-heads can find hotel info at the Netherlands Tourist Bureau's site:
*http://www.visitholland.nl*

**Hemp Hotel Amsterdam** - *Frederiksplein 15, 625-4425*
*http://www.hemp-hotel.com*

This little pension in the centre of Amsterdam is totally unique. The five small rooms, all decked out in hemp, each have their own theme. Try sleeping on a hemp mattress for a few nights in the Afghani room. Or, if you've always fancied a visit to the Himalayas, book the Indian room. Rates that include a vegetarian breakfast are ƒ100 for a single, ƒ135 for a double, and ƒ150 for a triple. Look for a drop of about 10% off-season. Downstairs, the bar has turned into a popular late-night hang-out. You can party there until 3 on weeknights and 4 on Friday and Saturday. They serve hemp snacks and - get this - it's the only place in the world with hemp beer on tap! Take tram 4 from Central Station to Frederiksplein. (Map area E8)

### Hotel Princess - *Overtoom 80, 612-2947*

This hotel is located at the corner of a busy intersection about a five minute walk from Leidseplein. It's a budget hotel with some nice touches like reading lights by the bed and mirrors. Single rooms are ƒ60-80. Doubles start at ƒ100 and go up to ƒ140 for rooms with a private shower and toilet. Triples are ƒ135-160. Quads ƒ160-200. You can request a double bed. Breakfast is included and it's excellent: bread, cheese, ham, cereal, boiled eggs, juice and coffee. The rest of the day, drinks and snacks are available at the reception. The staff are very nice. Take tram 1 from Central Station to Constantijn Huygensstraat. (Map area B7)

### Hotel Crystal - *2e Helmersstraat 6, 618-0521*

The owners of the Princess opened this hotel last year. It's also close to Leidseplein, but on a quieter street. Singles go for ƒ70-80, doubles without facilities for ƒ120-160. Doubles with shower, toilet, and TV go for ƒ140-180. Triples and quads are available, and all rooms will have TVs soon. An all-you-can-eat breakfast is included here, too. From Central Station take tram 1 to Overtoom and then walk two blocks along Nassaukade. (Map area B6)

### Hotel Abba - *Overtoom 122, 618-3058*

This is another hotel with friendly, helpful staff. An all-you-can-eat breakfast in a sunny room is included in the price. Depending on the season, singles cost from ƒ45 to ƒ75. Doubles (some with shower and toilet) range from ƒ80 to ƒ140. There are some triples, too. There's a nice view from the front (especially from the upper floors), but it can be a bit noisy because of the street. Most of the rooms have been refurbished, with phones and TVs added. If you're staying for awhile they have some two room apartments (for 4 to 6 people) with kitchens (no stove, though) for ƒ180-240. The free safety-deposit boxes in the reception area are a very nice feature: use them! Close to Leidseplein and Vondelpark. Tram 1 from Central Station to Constantijn Huygensstraat. (Map area A7)

### Get Lucky Guest House - *Keizersgracht 705, 420-6466*
*http://www.xs4all.nl/~getlucky*

The four cosy guest rooms in this old canal house have all been renovated recently, and at ƒ80 to ƒ125 per night for a double, they're a good deal. The location is great - close to everything - and most of the rooms have a beautiful canal view. The owners are more than happy to give you tourist info, or you can hang out in the comfy lounge (with free Internet facilities) and pick up some tips from other travellers. It's a good idea to call and book in advance because this is a popular little place. Take tram 4 from Central Station to Keizersgracht. It's right there. (Map area E7)

### The Flying Pig - *Nieuwendijk 100, 420-6822, Vossiusstraat 46-47, 400-4187*

Both these hostels have double rooms with shower and toilet for ƒ110. See the Hostels section for more details.

### Groenendael - *Nieuwendijk 15, 624-4822*

If you prefer to stay closer to the centre of town, then this hotel is a good deal. Singles go for ƒ60, doubles for ƒ95, and triples for ƒ135 (cheaper off season). Showers and toilets are in the hall. Breakfast is included. The rooms are pretty basic, but you're paying for the location. There's a comfortable lounge where you can hang out and meet people. From Central Station, walk or run. (Map area D3)

### Arena - *'s Gravesandestraat 51, 694-7444*

I already mentioned this place in the Hostels section, but I didn't say that they also have double and quad rooms, with shower and toilet, that are a good deal in low season, if you don't mind staying a bit out of the centre. Doubles go for ƒ135 (ƒ90 in low season). No breakfast is included. However, all rooms have reading lights by the beds: the mark of a good hotel. Quad rooms with shower and toilet are ƒ230 (ƒ160 in low season). There's a ƒ40 key deposit which is returned when you check out. Make a reservation. Close to the Tropenmuseum. From Central Station take tram 9 to Mauritskade. Night bus 76 or 77. (Map area G8)

### Hotel Aspen - *Raadhuisstraat 31, 626-6714*

Singles here start at ƒ55. A nice-sized, double room with shower and toilet costs ƒ120. Doubles with sink only are ƒ80-85. Triples go for ƒ140, quads for ƒ170, both with shower and toilet. No breakfast, but a great location close to Dam Square and Anne Frank House. From Central Station take tram 13 or 17 to Westermarkt and walk back half a block. If you don't have much luggage, it's only a 10-15 minute walk. (Map area C4)

### Van Ostade Bicycle Hotel - *Van Ostadestraat 123, 679-3452*

If you're travelling by bicycle take note. This is one of the only hotels in Amsterdam with free indoor bike parking. They also rent bikes to guests for ƒ7.50 per day and provide info on tours in and out of Amsterdam. The rooms? ƒ95-125 for a double with sink; ƒ130-155 for a double with shower. Breakfast is included. The rooms aren't exciting, but they're clean and all now have TVs. There's a library/lounge downstairs. It's close to the Albert Cuyp market. Follow tram 24 or 25 from Central Station to Ceintuurbaan and then go one block further.

### Black Tulip Hotel - *Gelderskade 16, 427-0933*
*http://www.blacktulip.nl*

I should start by saying that this hotel, situated in a 16th century canal house near Central Station, caters exclusively to leather men. That is, gay men who are seriously into S/M, B&D and leather fetish. Each of the nine luxurious rooms is decorated differently, but all feature kinky sex equipment: metal cages, stocks, fist-fuck chairs, etc. In addition to a sling and bondage hooks, all rooms have TVs with VCRs, minibars, telephones, and private bathrooms (some with whirlpool). Prices range from ƒ190 to ƒ310 and include a buffet breakfast in their comfortable lounge. And, as a service to guests who prefer to travel light, they rent big, heavy, leather boots and other paraphernalia here, too. (Map area E4)

*A bed at the Black Tulip.*

**Amstel Botel** - *Oosterdokskade 2-4, 626-4247*

It's not really cheap to stay at this 4 story, floating hotel, but if you've got a little extra money it's sort of unique to stay on a boat. The rooms are small, but very clean and modern. They all have a tiny shower and toilet, a phone, and a TV with free in-house videos and a movie channel. The reception is open 24 hours and they don't charge commission to change money. Rooms with a double bed or two single beds cost ƒ147-157; singles cost ƒ129-139. There are also some triple rooms. Prices drop ƒ10 in the winter. Breakfast is not included. Make sure you get a room overlooking the water. Located just a couple of minutes walk east of Central Station. (Map area F3)

# Hotel Strips

Walking around and looking for a hotel can be a pain, but if you really want to, here are a couple of areas with clusters of hotels, which should make it a little easier for you.

### Raadhuisstraat

The beautiful Art Nouveau "Utrecht Building", located just east of the Westerkerk (West Church), is full of small reasonably priced hotels. I stopped in at the Hotel Aspen (see above). These hotels fill up fast. (Map area C4)

### Warmoesstraat

You'll find several hostels and hotels here at the edge of the Red Light District. Some of them are dives and others, like the Hotel Kabul (tel: 623 7158) have been around a long time and have a good reputation. The Globe (Oudezijds Voorburgwal 3; 421-7424) is also popular. (Map area E4)

# CAMPING

**Zeeburg** - *Zuider IJdijk 20, 694-4430*

All kinds of new facilities have sprung up here recently, including a funky bar that has regular parties in the summer. Camping costs ƒ7.50 per person plus ƒ5 per tent. They also have a dorm room with beds that go for ƒ17,50 per person, and "camping huts" with beds at ƒ25 per person. Open all year. Take the metro to Amstel Station, then bus 37, and then it's a 2 minute walk. Night bus 77 or 79 (20 minute walk).

**Gaasper Camping** - *Loosdrechtdreef 7, 696-7326*

ƒ6.75 per adult, ƒ3.50 per kid, ƒ4 per dog (plus ƒ7.25 for a 2 person tent, ƒ9.25 for a 3 person tent, and ƒ6.25 per car). Open March 15th to December 31st. Take the metro from Central Station to Gaasperplein.

**Amsterdamse Bos** - *Kleine Noorddijk 1, 641-6868*

There's a campsite here in the beautiful woods just south of the city centre. ƒ8.75 per person, ƒ5.50 per tent, ƒ4.75 per car. Open April 1st to October 31st. Bus 171 from Central Station. Ask the driver for the closest stop.

**Vliegenbos** - *Meeuwenlaan 138, 636-8855*

ƒ14.25 per person. And you'll be charged extra if you have a vehicle. There are also 30 cabins (four beds each) that rent for ƒ80 a night. They accept written reservations for the cabins from March. Open April 1st to September 30th. Bus 32, 36. Night bus 73.

# GETTING AROUND

Central Amsterdam's old cobblestone streets are great for wandering through and getting lost. And fortunately, Amsterdam is full of people who speak English (to get you found). But, actually, you shouldn't have too much trouble if you take a few minutes to study a map. Detailed maps are available all over. Buy one: they're only ƒ4 and the street names listed on the back will make it easy to quickly find the places mentioned in this book. If you really can't afford to buy one, there are also a variety of free maps available around town: the Amsterdam Diamond Center (Rokin 1-5) offers maps of the city centre; both High View and the BCD (Cannabis Retailers' Association) produce advertising maps that are available in many coffeeshops; the Gay Tourist Map is free at COC (see Cafés); and at tourist locations you'll find a *Visitors Guide* published by the Yellow Pages that includes a pretty good map.

The basic layout of the city, with a series of horseshoe shaped canals surrounding the oldest part, makes it fairly easy to find your way on foot. This is certainly the best way to see Amsterdam and fully appreciate its incredible beauty.

## BICYCLES

Don't be scared to rent a bike and go for an authentic Amsterdam experience. Unlike most North American and many European cities, bikes are respected in Amsterdam. There are still too many dirty, ugly, polluting cars in the city centre, but there are also thousands of beautiful, clean, fast, efficient bicycles. There are bike lanes all over the city and it's a fun, safe way to explore. Listed below are several places to rent bikes. If you're here for awhile you may want to consider buying a used bike and selling it to someone when you leave. Make sure you lock your bike everywhere, even if you're only leaving it for an instant (see note on bike theft). The Waterlooplein flea market (see Markets, Shopping chapter) is the cheapest place to buy a lock.

*Buttman at a bike demo.*

In the 1960's Amsterdam experimented with a unique public transport project: white bicycles were placed around the city with the idea that anyone could use them for free. They were all stolen within a couple of weeks. Now a new "white bike" program is being prepared. The new bikes are very strange looking (instantly recognizable), very sturdy (with solid rubber tires), and will be locked to their depots around the city. Each depot will have a computer terminal (much like a bank machine) where you can insert a pre-paid card to unlock a bike. The cost will depend on how busy each station is: ride to a busy depot and you'll pay up to ƒ2.50, whereas a trip to an almost empty depot might be free. It's a pretty cool idea and it should get rolling sometime this year.

I've never been on an organized bike tour in Amsterdam, but if you're more comfortable riding with a group, Mike's Bike Tours (651-4275; *http://www.bavaria.com/mike*) does both inner-city and countryside trips.

The first Friday of every month *Autolozen*, a group of cycle activists, holds a Critical Mass type of bike demonstration to protest the large number of cars in the city centre. Everyone meets at 16:00 at Nieuwmarkt to take a slow, noisy, traffic-stopping ride through the city.

### Macbike - *Marnixstraat 220, 626 6964; Mr. Visserplein 2, 620-0985*

Good quality bikes and a good reputation. They also provide a free brochure with information on cycling routes outside the city. ƒ12.50 per day plus ƒ50 and passport, or else a credit card. Special weekly rate: ƒ60. Theft insurance (optional) costs an extra 50%. Open: daily 9-18. (Map areas B5,E6)

### Bike City - *Bloemgracht 70, 626-3721*
*http://www.bikecity.nl*

This is a genuinely friendly shop located on a beautiful canal near the Anne Frank House. Standard bikes cost ƒ12.50 per day (ƒ10 for each extra day) and the weekly rate is ƒ50. They also rent 3-speed bikes with hand-brakes (ƒ17.50 per day) and 5 speed mountain bikes (ƒ22.50 per day). If you ask, you'll also be provided with a puncture repair kit - a bonus if you're heading for the countryside. A cash deposit of ƒ50 and a passport are required. Open: daily 9-18. Closed in winter. (Map area B4)

### Rent-A-Bike-Damstraat - *Pieterjacobszdwarsstraat 11, 625-5029*

You'll find Rent-A-Bike in an alley off Damstraat just east of Dam Square. They're also very friendly. Keep your eyes peeled for their small coupons that get you a 10% discount. The only drawback to renting here is the big sign on the front of their bikes that scream "tourist". ƒ12.50 per day, but the more days you rent the cheaper it gets. Their special weekly rate is ƒ64.50. ƒ50 deposit plus a passport, or else a credit card. Open: daily 9-18. (Map area D5)

---

## A NOTE ON BIKE THIEF MOTHERFUCKERS

**Last year in Amsterdam over 150,000 bikes were stolen. Hot bikes are sold by sorry looking junkies who cruise around mumbling "fiets te koop", but more bikes are actually stolen by organised gangs. Junkies sell hot bikes very cheaply, but if you're tempted to buy one while you're here, think again. When you buy a stolen bike you're hurting the person who owned it, as well as keeping the asshole who nicked it in business. And I don't want to lose my transportation just because you want a cheap bike.**

---

### Take-A-Bike - *Stationplein, 624-8391*

Out the main doors at Central Station and to your left. Cheap, but kinda sleazy. ƒ9.50 per day. ƒ200 deposit. Special weekly rate: ƒ38. Open: daily 8-22. (Map area E3)

### De Rommelmarkt - *Looiersgracht 38*

If you're interested in buying a used bike, check the big tree by the entrance to this flea market (see Markets, Shopping chapter): sometimes there are a few up leaning against it. If you're lucky, you might find something for ƒ50-100. Wednesday and Saturday are the best days to look. Open: 11-17. (Map area B6)

**Binnenpret** - *1e Schinkelstraat 14, tel: 0651-720911*

Another place to buy a cheap bike is at the shop in a shed in the courtyard of this old squat. The guy who runs it sells very basic, refurbished bikes for ƒ80. He may have one on hand, but often you have to place an order and then pick it up later. Usually open mon-fri 12-19.

**Via Via** - *626-6166*
*http://www.viavia.nl/am/uk/beginner.asp*

*Via Via* is a classified ads paper that's published on distinctive yellow newsprint every Tuesday and Thursday. It features thousands of articles for sale and is available all over town. Look under *"Fietsen"*. There are always lots of cheap bikes listed, though you'll have to find a Dutch speaker to help you read the ads. The paper costs ƒ4.50, but you can peruse it at the library for free (see Hanging Out chapter).

# INLINE SKATES

**Rodolfo's** - *Sarphatistraat 59, 622-5488*
*http://www.rodolfos.com*

Inline skates for rent! Skating is not bad on the bike lanes and the people who work here at Europe's oldest skateshop know all the hot spots around town. The rental is from 12 noon to 11:00 the next day, and the price is ƒ15. A ƒ100 deposit and ID, or else a credit card is required. They also sell snowboards, skateboards, and skate fashions. Open: mon 13-18; tues-fri 10-18 (thurs 'til 21); sat 10-17. (Map area E8)

**Rent A Skate** - *tel: 06-54-66-2262*

Vondelpark is the best place to skate, especially if you're inexperienced and want to avoid auto traffic. Skates are rented by the café at the Amstelveenseweg end of Vondelpark, and by the café near the tennis courts in the middle of the park. You'll need ƒ7.50/hour plus a passport and ƒ50, or else a ƒ200 deposit. They're open (when the streets are dry) from May to October, daily, 11 to sunset; and on weekends from mid-March to May.

**Friday Night Skate** - *Vondelpark*

As long as the roads are dry, skaters meet every Friday evening at 20:00 in front of the Film Museum in Vondelpark and head out for a tour through the city. Everyone is welcome. For a comprehensive listing of this and other skate events, check out the excellent *Amsterdam Skate Page* on the Internet - *http://www.skate.nl/amsterdam.htm.* (Map area B8)

# MOPEDS

**Moped Rental Service Amsterdam** - *Marnixstraat 208-210, 422-0266*

Are you, like, born to be wild? But also kind and gentle? Then this place is for you. The rental includes insurance and a full tank of gas. One hour -ƒ12.50; second hour -ƒ10; third hour -ƒ7.50. Half day -ƒ35; full day - ƒ60. They rent scooters now, too. Open: daily 9-20 (summer); 11:30-18 (winter). (Map area B5)

# PUBLIC TRANSPORT

Most people visiting Amsterdam stay mainly in the centre and don't have to rely too much on public transit. But if you need it, you'll find there's a good network of trams, buses and metro lines. The transit system operates largely on the honour system, so you can try to ride for free if you want, but if you get caught the "I'm a tourist; I didn't understand" routine usually won't work. The fine is ƒ100 plus the fare. And by law you have to show them some ID. The same year that South Africa did away with its oppressive pass laws, Holland introduced one. Figure that out while the transit police take you away. It happens!

Amsterdam is divided into zones, and the more zones you travel in the more expensive your ticket will be. If you'll be using public transit for more than one round trip your best bet is to buy a 15 strip *strippenkaart* for ƒ11.75. Most of central Amsterdam is one zone. For each ride in the centre you must stamp two strips on your card. You can do it yourself in one of the yellow boxes you'll find in most trams and metro stations, or you can ask the driver or tram conductor to do it for you. Your ticket is then valid for an hour within that zone (the last in the series of numbers stamped on your ticket is the time you embarked). You have to stamp an extra strip for each additional zone you want to travel in or through - one zone costs two strips, two zones cost three strips, etc. Buy these *strippenkaarten* at Central Station, post offices, tobacco shops or some supermarkets. Single tickets can be purchased on trams and buses, but they're much more expensive (ƒ3). You can also purchase day tickets that are good on all buses, trams, and the metro (subway) from 1- 9 days (1 day -ƒ10; 2 days -ƒ15; 3 days -ƒ19; 4 days -ƒ23; 7 days -ƒ35). After midnight, night buses take over, but only on some routes, and the prices go up. To disembark your train, tram or bus, push the button by the door.

The "circle-tram 20" runs in a loop around Amsterdam, starting at Central Station and stopping at most of the major tourist sites. The day tickets mentioned above can be bought from the conductor on this line.

For more information and free route maps stop by the GVB (public transit) ticket office. Walk across the little square in front of Central Station and you'll find it on your left, next to the VVV. Open from April to late October: mon-fri 07-21:00; sat/sun 08:00-21:00; in winter 'til 19:00. You can also call 06-9292 for directions, but it costs 75 cents per minute and I've found that they often give bad advice.

# CARS

### Parking

There are already too many fucking cars in Amsterdam, but if you have to bring one into the city the best thing to do is put it in a garage and leave it there. It's expensive, but nowhere near as much as if you get caught parking illegally. The most convenient is probably Europarking (Marnixstraat 250, 623-6694). The winter price is ƒ2.75/hour, ƒ32/day. In summer it's ƒ3/hour, ƒ40/day. Open: mon-thurs 6:30-1:00; fri/sat 6:30-2:00; sun 7-1:00. ANVB Parking (Prins Hendrikkade 20a) costs even more - ƒ4.50/hour; ƒ45/day - but it's open 24 hours.

Parking on the street costs anywhere from ƒ2.75 to ƒ4.75 an hour depending on the neighbourhood you're in and the time of day. You pay at little blue boxes that are on every block, and the instructions are in English. I've been told that if you go a bit out of the city centre, for instance to the neighbourhood at the end of tramline 13, you can find free street parking. You'll have to research this yourselves.

**Warning:** wheel clamping of illegally parked cars is very common in Amsterdam. If it happens, you'll have go to an inconveniently located office to pay your ticket (about ƒ125!) and then wait for someone to come around and unclamp your car.

### Car Rental

If you want to rent a car, look in the yellow pages under *"autoverhuur"*. The cheapest I've found is Kuperus (Van der Madeweg 1, 668-3311), but the guys who work there are exceedingly unpleasant. It might be worth it to pay a bit more somewhere else. Note that If you can provide an Amsterdam address for the rental agreement, you might get a better deal from the major rental companies as some have special rates for residents.

### 24 Hour Gas Stations

There are gas stations open 24 hours at Sarphatistraat 225 and Marnixstraat 250. Please remember when you're buying gas that Shell Oil helped prop up the apartheid regime in South Africa. They also supported the corrupt military dictatorship in Nigeria that murdered Ken Saro-Wiwa and so many other Ogoni people. Shell isn't the only sleazy oil company around, but they are the target of a world-wide boycott. Hit the greedy bastards where it hurts them the most: in their pockets.

### Taxis

They're expensive, and they treat cyclists like shit, but if you really need one call 677-7777 and enjoy the service: taxis here are very comfortable. You can't flag one down on the street, but there are taxi stands at Central Station, Dam Square, Leidseplein, Rembrandtplein, Nieuwmarkt, Haarlemmerpoort, the Tropenmuseum, etc.

# BOATS

### Tours

Boat tours leave from several docks in front of Central Station and along the Damrak. It's very touristy, but I think it's fun to see the city from the canal perspective, and some of the taped info is interesting. The tours usually give you a quick look at the harbour and then cruise along the canals while a recording in four languages describes the sights. The routes vary slightly, last one hour, depart every twenty minutes or so, and cost about ƒ13. The canals are particularly beautiful at night. The last tours depart at 22:00 and are often sold out in advance.

### Motor Boats

Ahoy matey! In the summer, Sesa Rent A Boat (509-5050, *http://members. trepod.lycos.nl/pjsteinml/sloepen.html*) has motor boats that seat 6-8 people. And they're electric which means you won't be polluting the canals with oil and noise. The cost is ƒ80 per hour and you must provide identification and a ƒ300 deposit. Sesa has two locations: at Koningsplein near the flower market, and at Nieuwmarkt.

Canal Motorboats (422-7007) is another company that rents electric motorboats. These seat 6 and rent for ƒ65 for 1 hour; ƒ110 for 2 hours; ƒ150 for 3 hours; and ƒ25 for every hour after that. You'll need ID and a ƒ300 deposit. Bring some food and sit back: they don't go very fast. Located on Kloveniersburgwal (close to Muntplein). Both these rental companies are open - weather permitting - from spring to fall, 10-22:00.

## Ferries

Behind Central Station, you'll find free ferries that run to North Amsterdam every few minutes. You can take your bike on with you and it's a good starting point if you want to ride out into the countryside. Most of the bike rental places will give you free info about scenic routes.

## Canal Bikes

Canal bikes, 2-4 person pedal bikes, are all over the old city canals in summer and look like a lot of fun. Beck was paddling around on one the last time he was in town! They can be rented at several locations including in front of the Rijksmuseum and Anne Frank House. One or two people pay ƒ12.50/hour each; 3 or more people pay ƒ10/hour each. Deposit ƒ50. Tel: 626-5574. Open: in summer 10-21:30 daily; spring and fall 10-18:30.

# GETTING OUT OF AMSTERDAM

## BUS

A lot of people assume that trains are the only alternative to cars for travel in Europe, but Eurolines *(Rokin 10; Amstel Station, 560-8787)* has service to almost 400 destinations. I've had both good and bad experiences with this company, but they are much cheaper than the train. Check it out early because not all routes are served daily and they often sell out in advance. Keep in mind that border checks, especially going into France, tend to be a lot more severe on buses than on other modes of transport. Tickets can also be purchased at the International Lift Centre (see below) and many other travel agencies. You must have your passport number to buy a ticket. Rokin office open: mon-fri 9:30-17:30 (thurs 'til 20); sat 11-17. Amstel Station office open: mon-fri 7-22:30. (Map area D5)

## HITCHING

There is a lot of competition hitching out of Amsterdam in the summer, but people do give lifts. Hitching isn't allowed on the national highways. Stay on the on-ramps or in gas stations. You'll avoid hassles from the cops and, anyway, it's easier for drivers to pick you up. If you're heading to Utrecht, take tram 25 to the end of the line and join the crowd on the Utrechtseweg. How about southern or central Germany? Hop the metro to Amstel station and try your luck on the Gooiseweg. For Rotterdam and The Hague go by tram 4 to the RAI convention centre and walk down Europaboulevard until you see the entrance to the A2 highway. Good luck.

**International Lift Centre** - *Oudezijds Achterburgwal 169, 622-4342*

The Lift Centre serves as an intermediary between drivers and passengers looking for lifts. They are affiliated with Lift Centres all over Europe and should definitely be checked out as an alternative to the bus or train. To use the service you must become a member, which costs ƒ10 and is valid for one year. Note that this fee includes insurance - a good deal. If you have a car and want to take on passengers in order to cut costs call 622-4230. Open: mon-fri 13-18; sat 11-15. (Map area E5)

## TRAVELLERS' BULLETIN BOARD

If you're looking for a companion to travel with through other parts of the world, check the bulletin board just to the left inside the main entrance of the Tropenmuseum (see Museum chapter). It's a great source of information. There are also ads from people looking for others to share the driving and cost of gas to points in Africa and the Middle East. (Map area H7)

## AIR TRAVEL

### Budget Travel Agencies

The NBBS is the official Dutch student travel agency and, despite the rude staff I've encountered at some of their shops, is worth checking out if you're looking for an air ticket. There's an info line (620-5071) or else you can stop by their office at Rokin 66, just south of Dam Square. But either way, be prepared to wait. There are several other budget travel agencies in the same area as this NBBS office. Budget Air is at Rokin 34 (627-1251), and for last minute deals (mostly to southern Europe and North Africa) pop into L'tur at Rokin 40 (421-1583). I had a good experience recently at D-reizen (Linnaeusstraat 112; 665-4840), which is part of a big chain. They've got great last minute deals with Lufthansa for two people travelling together. World Ticket Center (Nieuwezijds Voorburgwal 159, 626-1011) sometimes have good specials and the consultants there are very nice. For a complete listing of travel agencies look in the phone book (the white pages) under "*Reisbureau*". Shop around.

**Airhitch** - *(via Point to Point Travel) Prinsengracht 230, 626-3220*
*http://www.airhitch.org*

With Airhitch, US and Canadian passport holders can buy stand-by tickets to a number of North American cities. Prices start at US $159 to the east coast (Montreal, New York City), $235 to the south and midwest (Toronto, Chicago, Miami, Tampa, and Denver), and $275 to the west coast (Vancouver, Seattle, LA, and San Francisco). At the moment you can fly out of a number of European cities, including Luxembourg, Paris and London. By summer they might have flights out of Amsterdam again, too. Open: mon-fri 9-17:30; sat 10-14.

**Call and Go** - *tel: 023-567-4567*

This phone line (run by the Dutch airline, KLM) is updated daily with good deals on next-day departures to all sorts of destinations. The recorded message is in Dutch and English. If you stay on the line after the message ends, you'll be connected with KLM reservations. Unfortunately, there are only return tickets on offer and the maximum stay is 4 weeks. Open: daily 13-23.

# GETTING TO THE AIRPORT

### Train

Easy as pie! Hop on the train at Central Station (f6.50) and you're at Schiphol Airport (*http://www.schiphol.nl*) in about 20 minutes. Trains depart daily, about every 10 minutes, from 5:12 in the morning 'til just after midnight. Then there's one train an hour starting at 00:42. (Did you know that Schiphol Airport is five metres below sea level?).

### Bus

The Interliner Bus rides between Leidseplein and the airport from about 5:30 to about midnight every day and costs f5.50 one-way, and f9 return. Call 0900-9292 (75 cents a minute) for departure times. It's a bit cheaper than the train, but then you have to spend a guilder on the phone getting the information!

# MAPS & TRAVEL BOOKS

**Pied à Terre** - *Singel 393, 627-4455*
Open: mon-fri 11-18 (thurs 'til 21, apr 1- sept 1); sat 10-17. (Map area C5)

**à la Carte** - *Utrechtsestraat 110-112, 625-0679*
Open: tues-fri 10-18 (in summer, thurs 'til 21); sat 10-17. (Map area E7)

**Geografische Boekhandel Jacob van Wijngaarden** - *Overtoom 97, 612-1901*
Open: mon 13-18; tues-fri 10-18 (thurs 'til 21); sat 10-17. (Map area A7)

**Evenaar** - *Singel 348, 624-6289*
(See Books & Magazines, Shopping chapter) Open: mon-fri 12-18; sat 11-17.

# GETTING TO THE BEACH

Trains to Zandvoort (on the coast), leave from Central Station approximately every half hour. On sunny days they are very crowded. The trip takes about 30 minutes and costs ƒ8.50 one-way and ƒ14 return. You can bring your bike for an extra charge (ƒ17.50), but unless you're planning to ride it back, it's cheaper to rent one there. Zandvoort can get very crowded, the water isn't exactly clean, and it's often very windy. But the beach is big, wide and white, and a day trip there can be a lot of fun. For the past couple of years, the hot party place to hang has been at Woodstock Beach, at Bloemendaal aan Zee, a 45 minute walk north along the beach from Zandvoort. It's a techno scene and a meat market, but it can also be a relaxing place to kick back, listen to the music and watch the sunset. Next door, at Solaris, they've also been having some pretty good parties. Sometimes there's a beach-shuttle that'll take you there for about ƒ3, but usually you have to hoof it along the beach. Remember to check the departure time of the last train back to Amsterdam!

# PRACTICAL SHIT

## TOURIST INFO

The VVV (pronounced "fay, fay, fay") is Holland's official tourist agency. However, it's also a privately-run business, so even though the people working here are almost always patient and friendly, and can be very helpful, you can see that the word from on high is "sell, sell, sell". They also have a bullshit policy of not giving out coffeeshop information (although they'll happily provide you with the address of any other business in Amsterdam). There's a branch inside Central Station, upstairs on platform 2 (open: mon-sat 8-20; sun 9-17). The main office is just to the left as you cross the square in front of the station (open: daily 9-17). There's also a branch at Leidseplein (open: mon-sat 9-19; sun 9-17). Be prepared for a long wait if you're here during high season. They have an info number, but it's very expensive (0900-400-4040; mon-fri 9-17; $f$1 per minute; *www.vvv.nl*). (Map area E3)

## MONEY

The **Dutch currency** is the guilder and it's represented by any one of these abbreviations: NLG, Hfl, or $f$. Coins come in annoying little 5 and 10 cent pieces (which you can get rid of in the candy machines in Central Station), 25 cents, 1, 2.50, and 5 guilders. Notes start at 10 guilders. Some shops are starting to list prices in euros ($€$) in addition to guilders, but the euro - the new single currency of the European Union - won't actually be in circulation until 2002.

I hate fucking banks! They're all thieves and scum. That 1% surcharge you paid on your travellers cheques? Pure profit. They're already paid by the cheque companies to sell them! Then they've got the nerve to charge you commission when you cash them. However, **changing money** in the tourist areas (like Leidseplein) is mostly a big rip-off, too: high commission charges and low rates. Beware of places that advertise "no commission" in big letters followed by fine print that says "if you're purchasing" (this means if you're giving them guiders to buy US $, for example). It's a scam, and once they have your money inside their bullet-proof glass booth you won't get it back.

**Pott-Change** - *Damrak 95, 626-3658; Rembrandtplein 10*

As we go to press, this place seems to be offering the best deals. They charge no commission to change cash and only $f$2.50 to cash non-European travellers cheques. Open: mon-sat 8-20; sun 9-20. (Map area D4)

**American Express** - *Damrak 66, 504-8777*

Amex doesn't charge a fee to cash their own travellers' cheques. Open: mon-fri 9-17; sat 9-12. (Map area D4)

**Thomas Cook** - *Damrak 1, 620-3236*

They'll cash their own cheques free of charge, but they charge a *minimum* of $f$7.50 to exchange cash, so watch out. Open: mon-sat 8-20; sun 9-20. (Map area E3)

**GWK Bank** - *Central Station, 627-2731*

This place charges 4.5% commission on the total amount changed - a rip-off - but they're open all night. (Map area E3)

# PHONE

Phone booths have instructions in English and for local calls you'll have to insert two 25 cent pieces. It's getting more and more difficult to find pay phones on the street that take coins: most take **phone cards**. However, many bars and restaurants have cash-operated ones. You'll need two 25 cent pieces for a local call. If you'll be making a lot of calls you might want to buy a phone card. They can be purchased in denominations of ƒ10 and ƒ25 at the VVV, post offices, tobacco shops, and supermarkets.

For **long distance calls** dial 00, then your country code and the number. Holland's country code is 31. Amsterdam's city code is 20. Long-distance phone cards are available in most of the "call centres" on tourist strips like the Damrak, and at tobacco shops. They come in denominations of ƒ25 and ƒ50 and they're a very good deal. Easy to use instructions, in English, are on the back of the cards. The best one I've found so far is issued by Telforte Atlas.

# POST

The **main post office** is at Singel 250 (556-3311) at the corner of Raadhuisstraat, just west of Dam Square. Turn to your left inside the main entrance and take a number: no pushing, no shoving. The system here is very efficient and the people behind the counter speak English (like most Amsterdammers) and are genuinely friendly and helpful. Post-cards take ƒ1 stamps. Letters up to 20 grams cost ƒ1 for Europe and ƒ1.60 overseas. In the same room are telephones, a photo-copier, a fax machine, and a passport photo booth. I like this place. The room to the right of the main entrance has a stationary store and a bank that changes money, but they're very slow and charge commission. The main post office is open: mon-fri 9-18 (thurs 'til 20); sat 10-13:30. (Map area C4)

The entrance to the **Poste Restante** is down some stairs to the left of the entrance to the main post office. If you're having mail sent to you the address is: Poste Restante, Hoofdpostkantoor PTT, Singel 250, 1012 SJ, Amsterdam, The Netherlands. Don't forget to bring your passport when you go to pick up your letters.

There are also post offices at Haarlemmerdijk 99, Kerkstraat 167, Bloemgracht 300, Waterlooplein 2. But note that their opening hours are often shorter than those of the main office listed above. For more postal info call the **free customer service line**: 0800-0417.

If you're posting letters from a **mailbox**, the right-hand slot is for Amsterdam, and the left side is for the rest of the world.

If you want to send or receive **e-mail** you can do it at The Mad Processor, Freeworld Internet café, or De Waag (all in Cafés) or the main library (see Hanging Out).

# LEFT LUGGAGE

The lockers at Central Station cost ƒ4 (small) and ƒ6 (large) for 24 hours. The maximum rental period is 72 hours at a time. If your stuff is too big for the lockers there is a left luggage counter that charges ƒ10 per piece for 24 hours. It's a rip-off, but what can you do? The maximum storage time permitted here is 10 days. Open 24 hours a day.

# VOLTAGE

The electric current in Holland operates on 220 volts. If you're from Canada or the U.S., you'll have to get a converter and/or a transformer if you want to plug in anything that you've brought with you. Note that converters/ transformers are probably cheaper in North America than in Holland.

# WEATHER

Expect lousy weather. Then if it's warm and dry, you'll feel really lucky (which you will be). Always bring layers of clothing and something waterproof. Umbrellas don't always do the trick, as this is a very windy country, especially in the fall. The North Sea wind also means that the weather can change very quickly and several times a day. Winters are cold, but it rarely goes below freezing. July and August are your best bet for nice weather (of course). Having said all that, Amsterdam is a fun city to visit any time of year.

# TOILETS

You often have to pay to use public toilets in Europe. There's usually an attendant on duty who collects the 25 or 50 cents required and who's supposed to be keeping things clean. It's not a lot of money, but it sure does piss me off (excuse the pun). A good place to find free and clean toilets are in expensive hotels. Just walk in looking confident and head straight in past the reception desk. There's always a washroom nearby.

# PICKPOCKETS

Amsterdam is a very safe city and the only crime you're likely to witness or experience is pickpocketing. It's not a violent crime, but what a drag when it happens! Watch out for these assholes: they're very good at what they do. Keep your valuables safely stashed and watch your bags at all times. The worst areas are around Central Station, Dam Square, Leidseplein, and the Red Light District - in other words, tourist areas where you'll probably end up at least a couple of times during your stay. Try not to act like a total space cadet (in spite of how you might feel) and you probably won't have any problems. (If you do, see the Phone Numbers chapter for the services you'll need.)

# DRUG TESTING

Hard drugs are illegal in Holland. Buying them from strangers can be dangerous. But if you've scored some ecstasy, call the Stichting Adviesburo Drugs (623-7943). *They do not sell drugs here.* It's a non-profit foundation that, among other things, will test your ecstasy to see what it really is. A test costs only ƒ5. They take a sliver as a sample (you won't lose your hit), and within a couple of minutes they can tell you what you've bought. This is a fantastic service (anonymous too, by the way). By testing ecstasy they know what's on the market, and if something bad is going around they can help track it down and get it out of circulation. They test cocaine, too, but it takes a couple of days. Open: tues-fri 14-17.

# FOOD

Eating out in Amsterdam is, on the whole, expensive. But if you listen to me and pay attention to this chapter I promise you a full belly at the best price.

If you're on the tightest budget, head to the markets for the cheapest fruit, veggies, cheese, etc. I've listed several in the shopping chapter. For dry goods go to the large supermarkets and remember to bring your own bags.

If you've got access to a kitchen you might want to visit a *tropische winkel* (tropical shop) for inspiration. They're found throughout the city, especially near the markets, and they specialize in foods from tropical countries: everything from mangoes to hot sauce to cassava chips.

## SUPERMARKETS

Supermarkets in Amsterdam are now open much longer hours than they used to be (in general: mon-sat 9-20; thurs 'til 21). More and more are staying open on Sundays, too. If you shop at Albert Heijn or Edah supermarkets, pick up a free, plastic "bonus card". You'll need it to buy anything on sale: without it you'll be charged the full price. It only takes about 30 seconds at the front counter (where they sell film, etc.) to fill out a short form with your name and address. Anyone can use the card - just give it to the cashier every time you check out.

**Aldi** - *Nieuwe Weteringstraat 26*
   This is one of the cheapest, but they don't have as good a selection as the bigger chains. And it's a bit hard to find.

**Dirk van den Broek**
   Another cheapie, but not so many locations in the centre.

   *Heinekenplein* - Big. American-style. Behind the Heineken Brewery.
   *Waterlooplein 131* - Right next to the flea market. Open Sunday.
   *Lijnbaansgracht 31* - In the Jordaan.

**Edah**
   Here are a few locations of this west-side chain.

   *Elandsgracht 118* - In the Jordaan.
   *Rozengracht 193* - Also in the Jordaan.
   *Westerstraat 100* - Again in the Jordaan.

**Albert Heijn**
   Every time I blink there's a new one. They have lots of organic products (look for green labels marked "bio"), and a number of branches stay open 'til late (see below). They're slick and well-stocked, but also expensive.

   *Nieuwezijds Voorburgwal* - Behind Dam Square. Open 'til 22:00 (sun 'til 19).
   *Koningsplein* - Open 'til 22:00 (sun 'til 19).
   *Haarlemmerdijk 1* - Ten minute walk from Central Station. Open 'til 22:00 (sun 'til 19)

*Vijzelstraat 117* - At Kerkstraat.
*Nieuwmarkt 18* - Just east of the Red Light District in the big square.
*Jodenbreestraat 20* - By the Waterlooplein flea market. Open 'til 22 (sun 'til 19).
*Westermarkt 21* - Across from the Westerkerk and the Homomonument.

# HEALTH FOOD STORES

**De Aanzet** - *Frans Hals Straat 27, 673-3415*

This pretty, cooperatively-run store is not far from the Albert Cuyp market (see Markets, Shopping chapter). They stock some bulk products, organic fruits and veggies, and yummy baked goods. Open: mon-fri 9-18; sat 9-17.

**Weegschaal** - *Jodenbreestraat 20, 624-1765*

You'll find all kinds of delicious, healthy foods in this neighbourhood shop, from macrobiotic products, to organic fruit and veggies, to taco chips. The people who work here are very friendly. It's just around the corner from the Waterlooplein market (see Shopping chapter). Open: mon-fri 9-18; sat 9-17. (Map area E6)

**De Natuurwinkel** - *Weteringschans 133, 638-4083 (also: Huidenstraat 19; Haarlemmerdijk 174; 1e Constantijn Huygensstraat 49; 1e van Swindenstraat 30)*

Health food, supermarket style. A huge selection including organic produce, cheese, and baked goods. Big, busy bulletin board. Weteringschans branch open: mon-fri 7-20 (thurs 'til 21); sat 7-20; sun 11-18. (Map area D8)

**Gimsel** - *Ferdinand Bolstraat 122, 624-8087*

This store is located on a busy street near the Albert Cuyp Market. It has a selection of whole grain breads as well as all the other healthy stuff. Open: mon-fri 9-19 (thurs 'til 20); sat 9-18.

**Natura Oase** - *Jan Pieter Heijestraat 105, 618-2887*

If you're in Vondelpark and you need some picnic fixin's, stop by this neighbourhood health food store. Bring an empty bottle because they also have organic wine on tap. Open: mon-fri 8-18; sat 8-17.

**De Spruitjes** - *Paleisstraat 137, 626-0076*

This building is "legal" now, but it's one of several in this neighbourhood around the Dam that was squatted a long time ago. It's central location makes it a convenient place to pick up some fruit to nosh on while you stroll. Anything marked with a green card is organic. This is a much nicer place to shop for produce than the big supermarket across the street. Open: mon-fri 9:30-18:30; sat 9:30-18. (Map area D5)

# STREET FOODS

Scattered around the city are **falafel & shoarma** take-aways, where prices start at ƒ4.50 to ƒ6. For shoarma try the Damstraat (just east of Dam Square), where there's a whole row of these places. Make sure you specify "small" if that's what you want or they'll try to give you a large and embarrass you into paying for it. For the best deal on falafels go to Falafel Dan (see Restaurants, this chapter), or Maoz Falafel (Reguliersbreestraat 41, by Rembrandtplein; Leidsestraat 85). They give you the pita and falafel balls and you help yourself to the rest. All you can pile on for ƒ6. Burp!

For **french fries** ("chips" to you Brits) try any place that advertises *vlaamse frites* (Flemish fries). These are the best. There is a large choice of toppings, but get mayonnaise for the Dutch experience. There's one at Damrak 42. There's also a good one on the Korte Leidsedwarsstraat north of Leidsestraat (near Leidseplein) and, maybe the best of all, at Voetboogstraat 33 (which runs parallel to the Kalverstraat). A small is usually ƒ2 to ƒ2.50, plus ƒ.50 each for a big selection of sauces. The cheapest fries in town are at Pizza Slice (Albert Cuypstraat 89) which has vlaamse frites with no sauce for only ƒ1! Delicious.

Fish lovers should definitely try snacking at one of the herring stalls that are all over the city. They're easily recognizable by their fish flags. All kinds of **fish and seafood** sandwiches are available from ƒ2.75. There is one close to Central Station on the bridge where the Haarlemmerstraat crosses the Singel canal and another next to the Westerkerk. Or for authentic British - read "extremely greasy" - fish and chips, try Al's at Nieuwendijk 10.

Another good bet for cheap food is **Indonesian or Surinamese** take-away. A big roti meal will cost you about ƒ6-7. A large plate of fried rice with chicken and pork runs about ƒ9-10 and is often enough for two people. For the best deal, though, see Restaurants, this chapter.

For relatively cheap **Chinese** take-away look around the Zeedijk (off of Nieuwmarkt) where there's a small Chinatown. And at the markets don't forget to try the cheap and addictive Vietnamese *Loempias* (spring rolls): veggie or meat, ƒ1-1.25.

**Sushi** is never cheap, but Tokio Sushi (Utrechtsestraat 98, 638-5677; Haarlemmerdijk 28) serves up some beautiful take-away at ƒ2.75 per piece, or ƒ15 for 6 pieces. Lots of varieties, including 6 veggie options and, on Utrechtsestraat, a rude guy behind the counter. Open: mon-sat 12-21.

Febo is the name of a chain of gross automats that you'll see all over the city. Here you can get **greasy**, deep-fried snacks for a guilder or two. In my opinion, your best bet is the *kaas* (cheese) *soufflé*. Here are a few locations: Damrak 6 (just down from Central Station); Kalverstraat 142; Nieuwendijk 220. They're open every night 'til 3.

While I hate American franchises like Planet Hollywood (I find it ironic that they tore down Amsterdam's oldest cinema to make way for an overpriced restaurant whose decor pays homage to movies), I was very happy to see Ben & Jerry's open in Amsterdam (Leidsestraat 90, and platform 1 in Central Station). Great **ice cream**. Leidsestraat shop open: daily 11-1:00 in summer; wed-sun 11-18 in winter.

The cheapest **soft drinks** in town are at the Virgin Megastore (Magna Plaza, Nieuwezijds Voorburgwal 182). Buy them at the vending machine for only ƒ1 as opposed to ƒ2.50 everywhere else.

**Pizza slices** in Amsterdam were my idea, damn it, and now they're everywhere (see All Night Eating).

# NIGHT SHOPS

"Night Shops" are the only places to buy groceries after the supermarkets close and are accordingly expensive. Fruit and veggies at these shops are a rip-off, but all the usual junk foods are available. Most night shops are open daily from 16:00 to 1:00. After that, you're fucked. However, a new law may soon license some to stay open all night. Here are a few in the centre.

**Pinguin Nightshop** - *Berenstraat 5.* Between the Prinsengracht and the Keizersgracht. (Map area C5)

**Big Bananas** - *Leidsestraat 73.* This night shop does a lot of business because of its location, but what a grumpy bunch. (Map area C6)

**Avondmarkt** - *de Wittenkade 94.* West end. Best selection and prices. (Map area B2)

**Sterk** - *Waterlooplein 241.* This place has cold-cuts, salads and cheeses too. (Map E6)

**Baltus T** - *Vijzelstraat 127.* (Map area D7)

**Dolf** - *Willemsstraat 79.* In the Jordaan. (Map area C2)

**Texaco** - *Sarphatistraat 225; Marnixstraat 250.* Open 24 hours. Eat here and get gas. (Map areas H6, B5)

# ALL NIGHT EATING

**Dalia Snackbar** - *Oude Hoogstraat 21*

It's not exactly a happening place, but all kinds of cheap meals are available here 'til late at night. Open: weekdays 'til 3; weekends 'til 4. (Map area E5)

**De Prins** - *Weteringschans 1*

Situated right across the street from the Paradiso (see Music chapter). Open: sun-thurs 'til 3; fri/sat 'til 4. (Map area C7)

**Bojo** - *Lange Leidsedwarsstraat 51*

This Indonesian restaurant (see Restaurants in this chapter) is open Saturday and Sunday until 4 and weeknights until 2. It's a good place for a late night pig-out. (Map area C7)

**Gary's Late Nite** - *Reguliersdwarsstraat 53, 420-2406*

Visit this little shop (see Cafés), in the wee hours for fresh muffins, cookies, and even bagels. Open: sun-thurs 'til 3; fri/sat 'til 4. (Map area D6)

**Febo Snackbars** - *all over*

I can't really recommend this shit, but they're open late and they're cheap (see Street Food in this chapter). Do what you gotta do.

**New York Pizza** - *Leidsestraat 23, Reguliersbreestraat 15, Damstraat 24*

Pizza slices until 1 on weekdays and 4 on weekends.

# BREAD

**Le Marché** - *Kalverstraat 201; Rokin 160*

The best bread in town. Open: mon-sat 10-19 (thurs 'til 21); sun 12-18. (Map area D6)

**Bakker Arend** - *Plantage Doklaan 8-12*

Once a week, this squat (see Live Music/Party Venues, Music Chapter) fills with the delicious smell of fresh bread made with organic ingredients. Also on offer are pizzas, cookies, and other yummy stuff. When you enter the building, the bakery is through the first door on the left. Open every Wednesday from 12 to 20:00. (Map area F6)

**Bakery Paul Année** - *Runstraat 25, 623-5322*

Exclusively hearty, healthy baked goods are sold at this famous bakery. I know people who are addicted to their muesli rolls. Open: mon-fri 9-18; sat 9-17. (Map C5)

# FREE SAMPLES

I don't know how desperate you are but...
Stalls at the Organic Farmers' Market (see Shopping) are a great source of free samples. Some Albert Heijn supermarkets have free coffee - usually by the deli counter. Gary's Muffin's (see Cafés) sometimes have one or two baskets on the counter with samples of their goodies. And finally, it's not food, but the Body Shop (Kalverstraat 157) displays tester bottles of all their lotions, creams and perfumes. Just because you're travelling doesn't mean you should let yourself go.

# BREAKFAST

Breakfast is such a good meal, but if you're travelling on a budget you don't want to be forking out a lot of dough - especially so early in the day. If you can't find a hotel that includes breakfast (see Hotels, Places to Sleep chapter), then here is a selection of eating spots where you can get something for less than ƒ10. Most of the these places also have traditional English or American breakfasts, but not for under ƒ12-15.

For the record, an *uitsmijter* (pronounced "outsmyter") means bouncer, and it's what you serve your guests late at night just before you kick them out of your flat. It consists of an egg fried with cheese, ham or another meat and slipped onto a piece of toast. It's very Dutch.

Finally, before you order coffee please read the introduction to the Cafés chapter in this book. It might save your life (or at least ƒ2.50).

**Barney's Breakfast Bar** - *Haarlemmerstraat 102, 625-9761*

Psssst. This is also a coffeeshop so you can get stoned while you munch. English is happily spoken and b-fast is served all day. A huge bowl of muesli, yoghurt, and 7 kinds of fruit goes for ƒ9.50. Three eggs on toast with melted cheese is also ƒ9.50. Coffee is served in a big cup. The food's not the best and the music is played too loud, but it's a pleasant atmosphere nonetheless, and they've done a really nice job with their recent renovations. It's located on an interesting shopping street. Open: daily 7-20 in summer; 8-20 in winter. (Map area D3)

**Winkel Lunchcafe** - *Noordermarkt 43, 623-0223*

If you're visiting one of the markets by the Noorderkerk on Saturday or Monday morning (see Markets, Shopping chapter) be sure to stop in at this very popular café on the corner of the square. They have one of the best apple cakes in Amsterdam. Everyone gets a piece and sits outside drinking cappuccino or fresh orange juice at shared tables along the crowded Westerstraat. It costs ƒ4.75, but the slices are big and you'll feel stuffed. Open: mon-sat 7-18. (Map area C3)

**Dimitri's Café** - *Prinsenstraat 3, 627-9393*

Dimitri's is located on a very pretty street between two canals. The boring music aside, it's a comfortable place to drink a pot of tea (ƒ3.50) and read the paper while you wait for your breakfast. They've got yoghurt and muesli for ƒ4.50, and until noon you can get a big breakfast for ƒ10.50. If it's too crowded, try the little place across the street. Open: daily 8-22. (Map area C3)

**De Gesmeerde Bliksem** - *Plantage Doklaan 8-12*

Every Sunday the cooks at this squatted building dish out an impressive all-you-can-eat breakfast for only ƒ5.50. You can expect fruit, salads, baked goods, scrambled tofu and other veggie eats. A wood-burning stove heats the room in winter, and by late in the day it can get pretty crowded with people who've settled in for a leisurely afternoon of food, conversation and tunes. Parties and art exhibits are hosted here, too (see Live Music/Party Venues, Music chapter). The breakfast café is open on Sunday from noon 'til 17:00. (Map area F6)

# RESTAURANTS

**Albert Cuyp 67** - *Albert Cuyp 67, 671-1396*

Surinamese and Chinese. What a deal! This little restaurant lies between two others that have basically the same menu, but this was the first one I tried, so I usually go here. Big portions for a low price. Try the roti kip (curried chicken, potatoes, cabbage, egg, and a roti) for only ƒ5.50! There are plenty of choices for vegetarians too. Meals run from ƒ5.50 to ƒ13 and don't be shy to ask what's what. Excellent banana chips. Located near Albert Cuyp Market. Open: daily 12-22:30.

**Vliegende Schotel (Flying Saucer)** - *Nieuwe Leliestraat 162, 625-2041*

Vegetarian. This restaurant is situated in a beautiful neighbourhood called the Jordaan (pronounced "yordahn"), so make sure that you take a walk around before or after your meal. They have a big menu that includes some vegan dishes. Meals start at ƒ11, and half-servings from ƒ7.50. Soup of the day is ƒ3.50. Order at the back and leave your name. They'll run a tab for you and you pay as you leave. It's comfy and friendly inside, and the room on the left is non-smoking. The only problem here is that the service is very slow and they often run out of food. If you're in a hurry or are very hungry, make sure you show up early. Open daily from 17:30 to 23:30, but the last call for dinner orders is at 22:15. (Map area B4)

### Thaise Snack bar Bird - *Zeedijk 77, 420-6289*

Thai. If you've ever been to Thailand you'll like this place. It's got the atmosphere down pat, with Thai pop songs, pictures of the king, and orchids on the tables. A lot of Thai people eat here, which is a good sign of authentic cooking. Meals aren't super cheap (average ƒ16), but the food is always prepared fresh and it's delicious. Worth the walk through this sleazy, junkie-filled neighbourhood. Open: daily 15-22. (Map area E4)

### Falafel Dan - *Ferdinand Bolstraat 126, 676-3411; Nieuwendijk 28*

Falafel. Actually they have more than falafels here, but that's what I go for. ƒ6 buys you a pita full of delicious, freshly prepared falafel balls. Then you waltz over to the salad and sauce bar and cram as much as you can into the pita. For me, it's a meal. And get this, every day from 15:00 to 17:00 is happy hour: all you can eat falafel balls! They also have a great selection of fresh juices. The Ferdinand Bolstraat location is near the Albert Cuyp market and has seating in the back. The Nieuwendijk branch has no seating. It's near Central Station. Both keep serving until late. Open: mon-thurs 12-1; fri/sat 12-3; sun 13-1.

### Addis Ababa - *Overtoom 337, 618-4472*

Ethiopian. This is a great restaurant to go to with a bunch of friends. The food is served in the traditional way, on a giant platter, and everyone eats with their hands. The decor is lively and the owner is a really nice guy. There are several veggie dishes, and something for carnivores, too. A full meal and a drink will set you back about ƒ15 per person - not exactly cheap, but not expensive either. Open: daily 17-23:00. (Map area A7)

### Foodism - *Oude Leliestraat 8, 427-5103*

Everything. This funky little restaurant is on the same pretty street as Grey Area (see Coffeeshops, Cannabis chapter). They make wonderful soups, salads, sandwiches, and a delicious vegetarian pasta. It's also a nice place to have a leisurely brunch with some friends. Although it's open for dinner, I actually prefer it earlier in the day before it gets too smoky. Open: daily 10:30-22:00. (Map area C4)

### De Peper - *'s Gravesandeplein 118, 665-6696*

Vegan. This building used to be a part of the of the hospital next door. After sitting empty for some time it was squatted and now houses several studios, a bicycle workshop, and a great restaurant called De Peper. It's very popular so make sure you arrive when they open in order to reserve a meal. Find out how long you'll have to wait and then settle in with a drink or, if it's still light outside, take a stroll in the Oosterpark which is right across the street. The meal consists of a starter (usually soup) and a lovingly prepared main course. The ƒ10 price is cheap for healthy, vegan food. Dessert is an extra ƒ2.50. They only cook on three nights, but lately the bar has been open on Thursdays for performances. From Leidseplein, tram 7 or 10 (direction Javaplein) will get you there. Open: tues, fri, sun 18-23. (Map area G8)

### Midnight - *Jacob van Lennepstraat 271, 683-3241*

Indian / Surinamese. I wouldn't really recommend eating your meal inside this Snack bar, but the food here is excellent and they'll deliver to your hotel for just ƒ2.50 - or for free if your order is more than ƒ15. My current favourite is their huge vegetarian roti (mmmm, roti) that costs only ƒ9.50 and really feeds two. Their Indian dishes, like vegetable *kofte*, *saag paneer*, and *chana masala* (all ƒ10 each) are also authentically prepared and delicious. There's plenty for carnivores, too. It's just across the street from the Kashmir Lounge (see Coffeeshops, Cannabis chapter). Open: daily 14-24.

### La Place Grand Café Restaurant - *Kalverstraat 201, Rokin 160, 622-0171*

Everything. Occupying a couple of little seventeenth-century houses, this department store food court lacks the usual fast-food crap and atmosphere. Elegant little booths display a wide variety of beautiful fresh fruits and vegetables bought directly from the producers. They also claim that most of their meat is free-range. The menu changes daily and everything is prepared fresh. Here are some of the cheaper examples from the last time I was here: gorgeous sandwiches ƒ4-5, soup ƒ5.50, excellent french fries ƒ3.75, giant hot chocolate with whipped cream ƒ2.95. It's a good place to seek refuge from the crowds of the Kalverstraat and they actually have a non-smoking section. The bakery attached to this restaurant makes some of the best bread in Amsterdam. Open: mon-sat 10-21 (thurs 'til 22); sun 12-21. (Map area D6)

### Zaal 100 - *De Wittenstraat 100, 688-0127*

Vegetarian. There's all kinds of stuff going on in this building (which I think used to be a squat), but to find the food, go in the main doors and turn to your right. The first door on your right, just past the bar, is the one you want. Inside is a crowded, cosy room filled with tables and mismatched chairs. There are stairs in the hallway that lead up to a small balcony with more seating. It's perfectly acceptable to share a table if the place is busy. A full meal of soup (ƒ1.50), a big plate of food for the main dish (ƒ6), and dessert (ƒ1.50) adds up to only ƒ9. It's not a gourmet meal, but it is tasty and filling. You don't need to reserve, but you should show up early. Open: tues, wed, thurs 18-20. (Map area B2)

### Einde van de Wereld (End of the World) - *Javakade, KNSM Island*

Home-cooked. With a lot of hard work by volunteers, the lively atmosphere of this famous squat restaurant has been transplanted onto a boat! Step down into the hold of the ship and there's a bright, bustling room filled with great music and the smell of terrific cooking. Go early as they only serve until the food runs out. There's a choice of a vegetarian or meat dish for ƒ9-11 or a half plate (lots of kids here) for ƒ6. Dessert costs ƒ3. It's a good deal: the servings are huge and there's also bread and garlic butter on the tables. Drinks are cheap. Order your meal at the bar, leave your name, pay, and in about 15 minutes they'll bring you your food. In good weather, take your beer and sit up top, overlooking the water. The boat's name is Quo Vadis and there's little sign in front. You can take bus 32 from Central Station eastbound (it'll say "KNSM Laan" on the front), to the Javakade stop. Then follow the road to the left for a few minutes. Or

*Dining out at Einde van de Wereld.*

better yet, take a bicycle. AMP is also in this area (see Live Music/Party Venues, Music chapter). Einde van de Wereld is open only on Wednesdays and Fridays from 18:00. (Map area I3)

**Toscana** - *Haarlemmerstraat 130, 622-0353; Haarlemmerdijk 176, 624-8358*

Italian. I'm always complaining to visitors about how pathetic Amsterdam pizzas are. And this place is no exception. But, all their pizzas are half price and I love a bargain. The cheapest pizza is a thin, but big, margherita for ƒ5, which means you can have a pizza and a beer for about ƒ8.50. And even though I bitch a fair bit, it's not terrible pizza. "When the moon hits your eye, like a big pizza pie, that's *amoré*..." Open: daily 16-23. (Map area C2)

**New York Pizza** - *Reguliersbreestraat 17; Leidsestraat 23; Spui 2; Damstraat 24*

Pizza. Even though I'm not usually into fast food chains, this is about the best pizza slice in Amsterdam. Prices range from ƒ3.75 to ƒ4.95. Keep your eyes open for their discount coupons being handed out around town. There are only a few seats inside the Spui location, but if the weather is good, turn right out the door and walk one block until you see a small arched doorway on your right. The beautiful courtyard you'll find inside is called the Begijnhof and it's a nice place to stroll as you munch. The Spui location has shorter hours: mon 11:30-22; tues/wed 11-22; thurs-sat 11-24; sun 11-21. Other locations open: sun-thurs 10-1; fri/sat 10-3.

**Pannekoekhuis Upstairs** - *Grimburgwal 2, 626-5603*

Pancakes. Not having a pancake in Holland would be like coming here and not seeing a windmill. It's part of the Dutch experience. This tiny place is on the second floor of a very cute, very old house. They have an English menu with prices starting at about ƒ6 for a powdered sugar topping. A pancake with strawberries and whipped cream goes for ƒ10.50. Students get a 10% discount. Open: mar-oct, tues-sun 12-19. In winter: wed-fri 12-19; sat 12-18; sun 12-17. Closed in January. (Map area D5)

**Restaurant Susy Cream Cheese** - *Cliffordstraat 36, 682-0411*

Vegetarian. Every Friday night this community centre serves up a fantastic three course meal from a different country. The place is plant-filled and cosy, buzzing with conversation and soft jazz. The appetizer costs ƒ2.50, the main course ƒ7.50, and dessert ƒ2.50, making a complete meal ƒ12,50, but you don't have to order every course (of course). And a bottle of Grolsch beer is only ƒ1.75! Call in the afternoon to reserve or show up early. Bus 18 or tram 10 from Central Station. Open: fri 18-20:30. (Map area A2)

**Bojo** - *Lange Leidsedwarsstraat 51, 626-8990*

Indonesian. This place is in all the tourist guides, but a lot of Dutch people go here too because the servings are huge, the prices are reasonable (ƒ13-18), and they're open late. Skip the appetizers: they're not very good. They also have a stupid rule that if you sit outside they won't give you a glass of water. The food is pretty good here, but if you want a real Indonesian "rice table" (and they're excellent) you have to pay about ƒ40 per person. If you have the dough try "Cilubang" (Runstraat 10, 626-9755) where the food is fantastic. Bojo is open: mon-thurs 16-2; fri 16-4; sat 12-4; sun 12-2. (Map area C7)

**Voku** - *Frederik Hendrikstraat 111, 684-6437*

Vegetarian / vegan. Voku is short for *volkskeuken*, which means people's kitchen. The volunteers here have been cooking tasty meals at different squats around

Amsterdam for years. Some meals are better than others, but the food is always good and very filling. An appetizer, main course, and dessert costs only ƒ7 on Wednesdays when they cook vegan food, and ƒ6 on Thursdays when it's vegetarian. On other nights there's a soup kitchen for the homeless, so not only do you get a unique dining experience here, but you're supporting a good cause, too. Call in the afternoon to reserve, or else show up early. Open: wed, thurs from 19:00. (Map area A4)

### Café de Molli - *Van Ostadestraat 55, 676-1427*

Vegetarian / vegan. This place serves big meals twice a week at a cheap price. ƒ6 gets you a full veggie or vegan meal in a very basic, communal setting. Call the number above in the afternoon to reserve your meal. For a little more info about this squat see the Cafés chapter. Vegan food is cooked on Tuesday. Vegetarian on Saturdays. Meals are served at 19:00. Eet Smakelijk!

### The Atrium - *Oudezijds Achterburgwal 237, 525-3999*

Cafeteria food. This is a self-service student mensa with cheap meals from about ƒ6-8 (even cheaper for students). Outside of meal times it's also a pleasant place to grab an inexpensive cup of coffee and a croissant and to rest your feet a bit. Meals are served on weekdays from 12 to 14:00 and 17 to 9:30. There's another student mensa, Agora, at Roetersstraat 13, that also has cheap meals and a big non-smoking section. Same hours as the Atrium. (Map area D5)

## A NOTE ABOUT SQUATTING IN AMSTERDAM

If a building in Amsterdam remains empty for more than a year without the owner putting it to some use, it can be squatted. This law is meant to protect the city from speculators who sit on their property while prices rise due to the severe housing shortage.

That doesn't mean that squatters have an easy time taking over a building. The legal definition of occupancy is a slippery one, and it's difficult to have a building defined as vacant. In addition, a great deal of work is usually needed to make a squat habitable and often legal battles ensue.

I have a lot of respect for those who have chosen to live as squatters as an expression of their political beliefs. They are simultaneously working to preserve and create housing in this overcrowded city. Several of these organised squats have opened restaurants and clubs that are among the best in Amsterdam. Many of them live under imminent threat of being forced out by banks and developers. Going to these squats is a way of showing your support for a creative, co-operative way of living as well as your opposition to conservative pigs who care more about money than people.

### Keuken van 1870 - *Spuistraat 4, 624 8965*

Cafeteria food. It opened as a soup kitchen in 1870, and you can still get a very cheap meal here. Full course, meat-and-potato dishes go for only ƒ10. Soup of the day is ƒ3,50. It's close to Central Station. Open: mon-fri 12-20; sat 16-21. (Map area D3)

### Moeder's Pot - *Vinkenstraat 119, 623-7643*

Dutch food. It may be called Mother's Pot, but it's really Pop's Grill. Except for the kitchen, Pop doesn't keep the little place too clean, and it has an atmosphere of neglect. The food, however, is tasty and plentiful. Generous servings of authentic Dutch meat-and-potato dishes can be had for less than ƒ10. The vegetable plate (*not* suitable for vegetarians) is a great deal at ƒ7.50, especially if you're tired and hungry after a long day. Open: mon-sat 17-22. (Map area C2)

### Terror Kitchen - *Entrepotdok 98, 420-6645*

Vegan. What a great name! But there's nothing too scary about having a meal in this giant, squatted warehouse, especially if you're on the tightest of budgets. Admittedly, it's a bit grubby and cold in here, but the food is plentiful, the music is good, and at only ƒ4 a pop, you won't find a cheaper meal in the city. Lots of other things go on in this building too (see Live Music/Party Venues, Music chapter). Call to reserve in the afternoon. When you get there, climb the fire escape on the side of the building and bang on the door to get in. Terror Kitchen is only open every other Thursday at 19:00. (Map area G6)

### The Magic Kitchen - *Vlaardingenlaan 11, 669-2539*

Vegetarian. Volunteers cook up a meal here every night of the week. The food is a bit hit-and-miss, varying from plain to excellent, but there's always lots to eat and you won't go away hungry. It's a pay-what-you-can deal with the money going back into the kitchen. As a traveller, you should donate at least ƒ5. It's a pretty groovy atmosphere (see De Elf, Music Chapter). Food is served every night about 19:00. No reservations.

# CAFÉS

Amsterdam's cafés are plentiful, and are ideal places to hang out and get a feel for the city. Once you've ordered you'll be left alone to read or write postcards or vegetate for as long as you like. Don't be shy to ask to share a table if you see a free chair: this is one of the most densely populated countries in the world (16 million people) and table sharing is customary.

*Koffie verkeerd* (literally "incorrect coffee") is *café au lait* and if you order "ordinary coffee" you'll probably get an espresso. Tea is charged by the cup and extra water will be added to your bill. I don't know the reason for this dumb custom. Fresh-squeezed orange juice, which is commonly referred to in french - *jus d'orange* - is available in most cafés.

Many cafés also serve snacks such as *broodjes* (small sandwiches) and *tostis* (usually ham and cheese sandwiches squashed into a sandwich toaster). Prices start at about ƒ2.50 for a plain cheese-on-white-roll or tosti. Another popular item is apple cake with whipped cream. It's an incredibly delicious Amsterdam speciality that should definitely be experienced.

### Villa Zeezicht - *Torensteeg 7*

Even with their expansion into the shop next door, this remains a cosy café. The seats by the big windows are perfect for reading the paper and people-watching. In the summer there are tables outside and on the bridge. Prices have gone up a bit. Sandwiches are ƒ4-6. They make an awesome apple cake for ƒ5 (a meal in itself). Make sure to ask for whipped cream (ƒ1). Open: mon-fri 8-18:30; sat/sun 9-18:30. (Map area D4)

### Café ter Kuile - *Torensteeg 8, 639-1055*

This pretty café/bar gets very crowded in the day with students from the university. But at night, after the dinner hour, it becomes mellower. I'm talking candles on the table, Tom Waits on the stereo, and a warm buzz of conversation. It's a good place to shoot the shit with a friend. Open: daily 11-1; fri/sat 'til 3. (Map area D4)

### Backstage Boutique and Coffee-Corner -
*Utrechtsedwarsstraat 67, 622-3638*

Greg, one of the Christmas Twins (identical twins who were big stars back in the US), died not long ago, and he is missed by many, many people. But his brother Gary is still running the Peewee-esque café they built together, and its unique atmosphere endures. It's not really cheap, but this place is great! They serve coffees, teas, juices and an assortment of sandwiches and cakes. The bottom of the menu proclaims: "Mama wanted girls!" The walls are decorated with wild sweaters and hats that were designed and made by the twins. If you're lucky, you might even walk out with a souvenir postcard. Gary is super friendly and very funny. Open: mon-sat 10-18. (Map area E7)

**De Waag** - *Nieuwmarkt, 422-7772*
*http://www.waag.org*

Right smack-dab in the middle of the Nieuwmarkt is an old building that looks like a castle. It was actually a gate to the city, and before that, a weigh station built in 1488! Now there's a pretty café inside. The food's expensive, but they have a few free Internet terminals right by the front entrance. It's fun to have a drink and read about the history of the building you're in on their web site. Open: sun-thurs 10-1; fri/sat 10-2. (Map area E5)

**Freeworld Internet Café** - *Korte Nieuwendijk 30, 620-0902*
*http://www.cybercafe.euronet.nl*

I think it's pretty cool that you can go into this place and have a coffee or a beer, light up a joint if you want, and go surfing on the Net. The charge is ƒ2.50 for 20 minutes and you must buy a drink. If you've never been online before, wait until the guy behind the bar isn't busy and he'll help you get started. You can also send e-mail from here. Remember to check the Get Lost Publishing home page (*http://www.xs4all.nl/~getlost*) to see what's new! If all the terminals are busy, head to The Cyber Café across the street at number 19, or The Mad Processor (see below). (For free Internet access see Libraries, in the Hanging Out chapter, and De Waag, above.) Open: sun-thurs 10-1; fri/sat 'til 3. (Map area D3)

**The Mad Processor** - *Bloemgracht 82, 421-1482*

There's not so much available here in the way of food and beverages (they serve non-alcoholic drinks and there's a candy-filled vending machine), but the real reason to visit this cyber-centre is to surf or do some gaming. Their 17 computers, one of which is a Mac, are set up in two rooms. There's a nice view of the canal from the front room and the back room, though larger, is cosy and sociable. Printers and scanners are also available. Computer use costs ƒ2.50 for 10 minutes, or ƒ12.50 an hour. Open: tues-sun 12-24. (Map area D4)

**COC** - *Rozenstraat 14, 626-3087*
*http://www.xs4all.nl/~cocasd/pag700.html*

This café is in the home of Amsterdam's main gay and lesbian resource centre (founded over 50 years ago!). Its relaxed atmosphere and considerate staff make this a good spot to have a drink and find out about gay happenings in Amsterdam. Pick up a copy of the *Queer Agenda*, a free, bi-weekly listing of what's going on around town. The free English language papers *Gay News Amsterdam* and *Gay & Night* (*http://www.gay-night.nl*) are also available here. And grab the annually-updated *Gay Tourist Info* booklet, too. It's in English, free, and includes a sexy story. On Friday nights the COC hosts a mixed dance, and there's a women-only dance every Saturday night (from 22:00; admission ƒ5). The café is open: mon-sat 13-17. (Map area C4)

**Café Saarein** - *Elandsstraat 119, 623-4901*

This famous, old-school dyke bar used to be one of the few women-only spaces in town, but it was recently sold and, while it will remain a gay cafe, it will now cater to a trendier, mixed clientele. The neighbourhood and the building are both pretty and interesting, so it'll probably remain a pleasant place to stop in for a beer. (Map area B5)

### Café Vertigo - *Vondelpark 3, 612-3021*

This café has one of the nicest (and busiest) terraces in Amsterdam. It's located in the middle of Vondelpark in the Film Museum building (see Film chapter). In bad weather duck into the cosy, low-ceilinged café where on Sunday afternoons you can often hear live jazz. Sometimes there are slide shows at the back. Open: daily 11-1 (from 10 in spring and summer). (Map area B8)

### Greenwoods - *Singel 103, 623-7071*

An Australian opened this café almost 11 years ago and despite the fact that it's trendy, I still like it. It gets very crowded around lunch, but at other times it's a calm place to have some tea and a bite to eat. There aren't many places in A'dam where you can get a pot of tea (ƒ4.50). They also have bagels with cream cheese, tomato and lettuce (ƒ4.50), and selection of home-baked cakes and scones. Open: daily 9:30-19. (Map area D4)

### De Badcuyp - *1e Sweelinckstraat 10, 675-9669*

This former bathhouse was saved from demolition by activists in the neighbourhood. Now it's a "centre for art, culture and politics" that's run by volunteers. It's located in the middle of the crowded Albert Cuyp Market (see Markets, Shopping chapter), and in nice weather there are tables outside. Inside it's spacious and relaxed: newspapers are scattered around and art exhibits line the walls. The upper level gives you a good view of the crowds shopping in the market below. They have a bar that serves snacks and full meals (the meal of the day costs ƒ12.50). There's often live music, either in the café or in the hall upstairs where they host popular dance nights featuring salsa, funk, jazz and disco. Open: tues-thurs 11-1; fri/sat 11-3; sun 11-1. (Map area E8)

### De Tuin - *2e Tuindwarsstraat 13, 624-4559*

De Tuin is a spacious, inviting café right in the heart of a beautiful old neighbourhood called the Jordaan. It's a traditional "brown café" (so-called because of the abundance of wood). I like to explore the area and then pop in here for an orange juice and a sandwich. There are usually cool people hanging out and it's a comfortable spot to relax for awhile. The view of the Westerkerk tower from this shopping street is very photogenic. Open: mon-thurs 10-1; fri/sat 10-2; sun 11-1. (Map area B3)

### Café de Pels - *Huidenstraat 25, 622-9037*

This is another traditional "brown café" with a diverse clientele. Warm and welcoming in the winter, while in the summer tiny outdoor tables make for good people-watching on this quaint little street. It has an authentic Amsterdam ambiance. Open: mon-thurs 10-1; fri/sat 10-3; sun 11-1. (Map area C5)

### Gary's Muffins - *Prinsengracht 454, 420-1452; Marnixstr 121, 638-0186; Kinkerstraat 140; Reguliersdwarsstr 53, 420-2406; Jodenbreestr 15, 421-5930; http://www.channels.nl/muffins.html*

Muffin's, brownies, chewy chocolate chip cookies and yes, bagels. Go for the bagel with cream cheese for ƒ4. The Prinsengracht location, which is just off Leidsestraat, is the one I like better in nice weather because of the tables out by the canal. Otherwise, I go to Marnixstaat or Jodenbreestraat which are airier and more comfortable inside. They often have day-olds for ƒ1. Gary's Late Night on Reguliersdwarstraat is open during the day, but I often swing by when I've got the munchies in the middle of the night. The shops each have their own opening times, but it's generally mon-sat 8:30-18; sun 10-18. Gary's Late Night is open: sun-thurs 12-3; fri/sat 12-4.

### Bagels & Beans - *Ferdinand Bolstraat 70, 672-1610*
*http://www.bagelsbeans.nl*

The bagels here, for my money, are the best in Amsterdam. They're often served hot out of the oven. A plain bagel costs ƒ1.50; with cream cheese ƒ3.50. They serve delicious coffees too, but I can't handle the thick tobacco smoke that engulfs everything here, so unless their terrace is set up, I usually get something to go. Open: mon-fri 8:30-18; sat 9:30-18; sun 10-17.

### Lunchlokaal Wynand Fockink - *Pijlsteeg 31, 639-2695*

The quaint little courtyard where this café is located provides respite from the bustle of the Dam Square area. In the winter it's just a nice little hideaway. In the summer though, the trees and plants grow lush around the little tables, creating a wonderfully peaceful environment. It's not super cheap, but they have sandwiches from ƒ5.50, and soup of the day with bread for ƒ5. Go through the covered walkway by Leonida's chocolates on Damstraat and you'll find it. Open: daily 15-21. (Map area D5)

### Café de Molli - *Van Ostadestraat 55, 676-1427*

This is a volunteer-run squat café with an emphasis on politics. They frequently host theme nights with videos and speakers on subjects such as the role of Shell (those murdering motherfuckers) in Nigeria. On other nights it's just a mellow place to hang out and meet some people. Drinks are very cheap. Tea is free. They also have a feminist café every second Wednesday of the month where a vegetarian meal is served. Open: sun-fri 21-1; sat for dinner only (see Restaurants, Food chapter).

**Sarah's Grannies** - *Kerkstraat 176, 624-0145*

This big café has a relaxed lived-in feel to it. Plants, wood tables, a piano, and classical music make it a comfortable place to lounge awhile and write a letter. It's a lesbian hangout, but draws a mixed crowd. Breakfast, lunch and snacks are available. No alcohol. Changing art exhibits. Formerly known as Françoise. Open: tues-fri 10:30-17; sat 11:30-17. (Map area D7)

**De Jaren** - *Nieuwe Doelenstraat 20, 625-5771*
*http://cafe-de-jaren.nl*

I find the food overpriced here, but I like the spaciousness, which is unusual in this city and means that you can almost always find a seat. In the summer there are two big terraces with a terrific view over the Amstel River. Lots of intellectuals hang out reading books. I often stop in to use the toilet. Located between Waterlooplein and Rembrandtplein. Open: sun-thurs 10-1; fri/ sat 10-2. (Map area D6)

**Oibibio** - *Prins Hendrikkade 20-21, 553-9355*
*http://www.oibibio.nl*

What makes this café special is it's spectacular interior, much of which has been restored to it's original 1883 splendour. The rest of the building houses a New Age cultural centre that includes a sauna, a book store, and a Japanese tea room (see below). Explore a bit if you have time. Across the street and just west of Central Station. Open: sun- thurs 9-24; fri/sat 9-1. (Map area E3)

**Japanese Tea Garden** - *Prins Hendrikkade 20-21, second floor, 553-9355*

Located in Oibibio (see above). Enter the building through the main doors, and go up the stairway at the back. There you'll find the entrance to the Tea Garden. Take off your shoes before you go in. The beautiful, two-tiered garden is built around a waterfall. English menus are available and you can choose from a variety of teas (from about ƒ3.50 per pot) as well as Japanese food. It's very relaxing to sit on the cushions and drink your tea while soft Japanese music plays. The area is smoke-free and no cell phones or laptop computers are allowed. It's an oasis of calm in the midst of all the commotion of the central Amsterdam. Open: daily 12-19. (Map area E3)

**Café Latei** - *Zeedijk 143, 625-7485*

Do you ever wake up and think to yourself, "I feel like drinking a cup of coffee, then buying some organic olive oil and a piece of furniture"? Because this cute, split-level café's got all that and more. Along with light meals (try the goat's cheese tostis) and beverages, they sell old furniture, knick-knacks, and a variety of olive oils. The way everything is scattered about in this café creates the sensation that you're in someone's living room. It seems to be a place that moms like to bring their kids on their way home from school. Open: mon-fri 8-17; sat 10-17. (Map area E4)

**Manege** - *Vondelstraat 140, 618-0942*

I'd always heard that this horse riding school had a great café with cheap drinks and snacks. It's true. Vondelstraat runs alongside Vondelpark (see Parks, Hanging Out chapter). Walk through the arch under the huge lamps, and enter the school via the big doors. The café is through the door on the left, and up a grandiose stairway. There's a balcony with tables overlooking the training area, but if you find the horsey aroma a bit much, you can still see through the windows of the main room of the café. It was formerly very elegant and is now filled with cats. Tea and coffee are only ƒ1,50. Beer is ƒ2. Cookies ƒ1. If you're coming from the park, take the exit near the Film Museum. Open: mon-fri 8:30-1; sat/sun 8:30-18. (Map area A7)

### W139 - *Warmoesstraat 139, 622-9434*

This building, which was squatted a while back, has been turned into an art gallery. The space is huge - perfect for the regularly changing, multi-media exhibitions on display. There's no charge to visit. The café in here is a cool, if somewhat grungy, place to kick back for a bit before heading back out into the crowds of the city centre. It's best to go in the summer, though, as it gets quite cold inside in the winter. Tea and coffee are cheap, and they also serve wine and malt beer. Open: wed-sun 12-18:00. (Map area D4)

### Info Kafee August - *Frederik Hendrikstraat 111, 684-6437*

This is a volunteer-run squat cafe. You'll find coffee, tea, juices, and veggie snacks at cheap prices. It's a great place to find out about the squat scene and local left-wing political initiatives as they often feature speakers and videos. There's a whole wall of political 'zines and papers to leaf through, and information about other activities that take place here, like their restaurant (see Restaurants, Food chapter). August is open once a week, on Saturday, from 18:00 to 23:00. (Map area A4)

### East of Eden - *Linnaeusstraat 11A, 665-0743*

A spacious café right across the street from the Tropenmuseum (see Museum chapter). The seating is a mish-mash of couches and easy chairs and lots of light comes in through the high windows on two sides. It's warm and mellow and the only problem is that it gets very smoky. Non-smokers should visit this café in the summer when they have an outdoor terrace. Open: daily 11-1. (Map area H7)

### De Roos - *Vondelstraat 35-37, 689-0081*

If you're into "creative and spiritual growth" or alternative health care, this centre might interest you. It's located in an old house just north of Vondelpark and is home to a New Age shop, practitioners' rooms, and, of course, a café. Meals and snacks are available, and if the weather's nice you can sit in the garden. Check the bulletin board for info about events in the community or talk to the staff at the reception desk. De Roos occasionally hosts a smoke-free disco on Saturday nights. Open: mon-fri 8-23; sat/sun 9-18. (Map area B7)

### Het Koffiehuis de Markt - *Albert Cuypstraat 122, 662-0105*

If you're shopping in the Albert Cuyp Market (see Markets, Shopping chapter), pop in here to see where the market people hang out. The decor is 1950s Dutch. It's got an authentic, working-class-Amsterdam atmosphere, and it's cheap. Coffee and tea are only ƒ1.40. Soup is ƒ3.25, and they serve inexpensive sandwiches, too. Open: mon-sat 7-18.

# CANNABIS

If you like to smoke marijuana and hash, and come from anywhere other than the Parvati Valley, then you're in for a treat. In Amsterdam you can walk into any "coffeeshop" (a café selling grass and hash) and order a coffee and a joint; then sit back and smoke, listen to music, perhaps have a game of backgammon or chess - without the worry of being arrested. How civilized!

You don't have to buy weed every time you go into a coffeeshop, but definitely buy something: a drink or some munchies.

The weed here is probably a lot stronger than what you're used to back home. If you find that a friend of yours is too high or feels a bit sick, often a sweet drink (like a cola) will help. Just thought I'd mention that.

Almost all coffeeshops have a menu listing the types of smoke available and where each one is from. It's fun to try grass from different parts of the world, but I have to say that a lot of the *nederwiet* (Dutch grown weed) is spectacular. Prices are usually listed by the gram and the weed is almost always sold in ƒ10 or ƒ25 bags. So if, for instance, Haze #1 is selling for ƒ12 a gram, a ƒ10 bag will contain 0.8 grams. Some coffeeshops will let you buy smaller amounts, too. Don't be shy to ask to see the menu, it's there to make it easy for you. You can also ask to see the buds before you pay. Then relax while you roll and ponder the absurdity of North America's repressive and hypocritical "war on drugs", and how fantastic it is to be in Amsterdam!

**Attention:** don't buy anything on the street! You will definitely be ripped off!

**Warning:** Space cakes and *bon bons* (containing grass or hash) are sold in some coffee shops. They can be very strong, almost like tripping, so have fun, but be prepared for a long, intense high. Also keep in mind that they can take up to a couple of hours to kick in, so don't gobble down another one just because you don't feel anything right away................................ What?

# COFFEESHOPS

**Global Chillage** - *Kerkstraat 51, 639-1154*
*http://www.globalchillage.com*

Most nights find this "chill out lounge" full of stoned, happy people. The lighting, decor, and ambient music all work to create an atmosphere of, well... global chillage! This is one of the new wave of coffeeshops that offer more than just a place to smoke and hang out, but that are also works of art in themselves. This shop also has good prices on smoke. Try their Northern Lights, or splurge on the Warm Ears Moroccan hash. They've often got deejays spinning on an excellent sound system, and recent renovations include new murals, a wild, jigsaw puzzle floor, and more spacious seating. They also sell a funky, holographic shirt that makes an excellent souvenir (see page 101). This is one of the cooler coffeeshops in Amsterdam and it's fitting that it should be situated along the trendy strip of Kerkstraat just off Leidsestraat. Open: daily 11-24. (Map area C6)

## De Rokerij - *Lange Leidsedwarsstraat 41, 622-9442*
*http://www.coffeeshop-nl.com/rokerij.htm*

Who would guess that in the middle of this touristy strip there's a great coffeeshop? The decor in here rules! It's a mixture of Amsterdam, Asian, and cave motifs. The music is spacey, but not sleepy, and there are lots of comfortable nooks to settle into. It's a popular spot and you can tell that they have a lot of regulars hanging out. My only complaint is that they don't let you park your bike out front. Open: sun-thurs 10-1; fri/sat 'til 3. (Map area C7)

## De Rokerij - *Singel 8, 422-6643*
*http://www.coffeeshop-nl.com/rokenew.htm*

This Rokerij is one of the nicest coffeeshops in the Central Station area. There are African influenced murals on the walls, and low, cushioned seats. Just make sure that you don't sit under one of the spotlights that fade in and out from time to time: unless you're a bit of an exhibitionist, it can be very annoying to be catching a good buzz and suddenly find yourself on centre stage. You can buy your smoke at the little hut near the front door, and they also serve alcohol. Check the little blackboard by the entrance to see which nights they're offering freebies like tarot reading or foot massage. (For the record there's another, smaller, Rookerij at Amstel 8). Singel branch open: sun-thurs 9-1; fri/sat 'til 2. (Map area D3)

## Grey Area - *Oude Leliestraat 2, 420-4301*
*http://www.xs4all.nl/~greyarea*

Originally, this coffeeshop was Amsterdam's first hempseed restaurant. Now they only serve tasty morsels of the smokable kind. They have a very select menu offering some of the newest strains of weed around (including the original Bubblegum), and their prices reflect this exclusivity. But connoisseurs will definitely get a kick out of this place. The staff are friendly and welcoming, the little old street it's on is beautiful, and the organic coffee is served in a bottomless cup! Print the coupon on their web site and bring it with you for a free drink. Open: tues-sat 12-22; sun 13-22. (Map area C4)

## De Overkant - *Van Limburg Stirumplein 20, 686-8957*

When this neighbourhood shop in the west celebrated its 10th anniversary a few years ago, they hosted a giant street festival. The street signs were changed to names like Cannabis Square, bands played, there were hemp burgers, vapourizer hits, and a lot more. It also gave me a chance to check out their menu for the first time in years, which is why you're reading this now: great party, great menu. Their hash rules! They always have several things on sale, and they're patient and give honest advice if you're looking for something specific. Open: daily 12-24. (Map area B2)

## De Overkant Hortus - *Nieuwe Herengracht 71, 422-1949*

This new Overkant is located right across the canal from the Botanical Gardens (see Museums), close to the Waterlooplein market (see Shopping). It's a small shop, but the simple, uncluttered interior and the big windows make it feel airy and open. They offer the same high quality weed and hash as the original shop, though the selection isn't as large. Smoking a joint here and then exploring the Gardens is a great way to spend an afternoon. Open: daily 12-22. (Map area F6)

## Greenhouse - *Tolstraat 91, 673-7430*
http://www.greenhouse.org

A lot of effort has gone into the design of this shop and you should take time to admire the cool mosaics and other decor. Upstairs there are a couple of pool tables where they host regular tournaments. As far as smokables go, Greenhouse has placed in almost every category of the High Times Cannabis Cup, so indulge. It's located a bit out of the centre. If you don't have time to make the trek, check out one of its sister shops (see below). Open: sun-thurs 10-1; fri/sat 'til 2.

## Greenhouse Namaste - *Waterlooplein 345, 622-5499*

This was the second Greenhouse to open in Amsterdam and, like at the first, no expense was spared on the architectural design: the toilets alone took three months to complete! I particularly enjoy spending time here in the afternoon - sitting at a candle-lit table, listening to music, and looking out at City Hall through their big window. The Greenhouses have always had high quality, if somewhat expensive, bud. You won't be disappointed. Open: sun-thurs 9-1; fri/sat 'til 2. (Map area E6)

## Greenhouse - *Oudezijds Voorburgwal 191, 627-1739*

Wow! They've done it again. Before it opened, they had this shop completely renovated, or should I say "Greenhoused". It's spectacular. There are little lights that gradually change colour embedded in the walls, ceiling, and tables, and the washroom walls are encrusted with sea shells. If you like their buds, you can buy the seeds from their own Greenhouse Seed Company. Open: sun-thurs 9-; fri/sat 'til 3. (Map area D5)

---

### A NOTE ON DRUGS IN AMSTERDAM

Once again Holland leads the western world in progressive thinking and action: soft drugs like cannabis and hashish have been decriminalized for over 18 years. Small amounts of these harmless substances can be bought, sold, and consumed without interference by the police.

Trafficking in hard drugs is dealt with seriously, but addiction is considered a matter of health and social well-being rather than a criminal or law enforcement problem. The number of addicts in Holland, where they can receive treatment without fear of criminal prosecution, is much lower than other countries where the law is used to strip people of their human rights (not too mention their property).

Some member states of the European Union (especially France), are putting pressure on Holland to conform to their repressive drug laws. This has resulted in the introduction of new drug policies that, while still more liberal than elsewhere, reflect a regressive trend in the thinking of the Dutch authorities.

Cannabis College (O.Z. Achterburgwal 124, 423-4420, *http://www.cannabiscollege.org*) is a non-profit organization that formed in order to educate the public about the cannabis plant and all it's uses. The volunteers who run the college are also dedicated to bringing about an end to the insane and unreasonable punishments inflicted throughout the world on those who choose to use cannabis, for whatever reason. They're located in a 17th century canal house. Stop in to look at the exhibits and see what events are going on, and while you're there visit their garden in the basement. They ask for a donation of about *f*5 which is used to help fund the college. Open: daily 12-20 (possibly longer in summer; shorter in winter). (Map area D5)

**Kadinsky** - *Rosmarijnsteeg 9, 624-7023*
*http://www.channels.nl/kadinsky.html*

A hip coffeeshop with an area upstairs that's perfect for kicking back and smoking that first joint of the day. The music is often in an acid jazz groove, but it depends on who's working. Delicious cookies are also available. Located on a tiny little street near Spui Circle. Open: daily 10-1. (Map area D5)

**Homegrown Fantasy** - *Nieuwezijds Voorburgwal 87a, 627-5683*
*http://www.homegrownfantasy.com*

For years, this well-known coffeeshop has had a good reputation for both the quality of their weed and the relaxed atmosphere of the shop. They have a large, tasty selection of Dutch-grown grass and a couple of types of hash. They also serve pots of tea. I like it here best in the daytime when the light is soft and time just seems to slow... right....... down. Be sure to visit the toilet where the black light makes your teeth glow and your pee look like milk! Just around the corner is their sister shop, Homegrown Fantaseeds. Open: sun-thurs 9-24; fri/sat 'til 1. (Map area D4)

**Abraxas** - *Jonge Roelensteeg 14*

Recent renovations, which include clear glass floors on the upper levels, have breathed new life into this already popular and well-established coffeeshop. The three little floors of this old house each have their own style and ambience. Sitting in the uppermost room, for instance, feels like you're visiting an elf's treehouse. And from up there you can also see into the expensive and arty Supperclub across the

alley, which makes for an entertaining show in the evening. Several deejays work here, so music tends to be pretty good. It also gets very crowded, especially on weekends. Juice is overpriced at ƒ3.50, but tea is only ƒ2. Open: daily 10-1. (Map area D5)

**Paradox** - *1e Bloemdwarsstraat 2, 623-5639*

I have to admit that I haven't tried any of their smoke, but the Paradox serves up some delicious organic food! Their awesome fruit shakes are a bit expensive, but if you've got the dough they're a real treat. I recommend the Pan Galactic Gargle Blaster (ƒ7.50). A lot of English speaking ex-pats hang here, especially on Sunday afternoons when, occasionally, there's live music. The staff are friendly and the neighbourhood is beautiful. Open: daily 10-19. (Map area B4)

**YoYo** - *2e Jan v.d. Heydenstraat 79, 664-7173*

YoYo is a perfect place to spend a mellow afternoon reading or writing, while you slowly smoke a joint. The shop is spacious and airy, which is particularly nice if you don't smoke tobacco. As it's a bit out of the centre (near Albert Cuyp Market), you'll find good prices on their organically grown buds. Food and drink are also cheap: cheese tosti -ƒ2, tea -ƒ1.50, organic apple juice -ƒ2. Now if only I could take control of the stereo... Open: daily 12-20. (Map area E8)

**Het Ballonnetje** - *Roetersstraat 12, 622-8027*
*http://www.channels.nl/balon.html*

This is one for those of you staying at the Arena. You won't find many tourists here, as it's a bit off the beaten track: it's a good place to meet Dutch people. Het Ballonnetje is small and very cosy with wooden furniture and a tall palm tree. Upstairs, in the loft, there's a TV and a stack of games. It's a peaceful place to play cards on a rainy night. I'm not crazy about the dance music they play here, but that's just me. Make sure to take a look at their terrarium housing tiny fluorescent frogs! Open: daily 10-24. (Map area F7)

**La Tertulia** - *Prinsengracht 312*

Plants, flowers and a little fountain give this coffeeshop a tropical feeling, but what I like best about this place is the outdoor terrace they set up in the summer. It's right at the edge of the canal and there are flowers on all the tables. It's easy to find this building: just look for the Van Gogh sunflowers painted all over it. Open: tues-sat 11-19. (Map area C5)

**Katsu** - *1e Van Der Helststraat 70, 675-2617*

Katsu is a long-standing neighbourhood coffeeshop located just off the Albert Cuyp Market. It's got a shabby, homey feel to it, and some wicked grass. They're famous for their Hazes which give a wonderful cerebral high. Well worth a visit. Open: mon-thurs 11-23; fri/sat 11-24; sun 12-23.

**Pi Kunst And Koffie** - *2e Laurierdwarsstraat 64, 622-5960*

An attractive coffeeshop/gallery in the Jordaan with big windows and lots of local art. The main floor has a big bar where you can buy smoke, drinks and snacks. Feel free to use the chess and backgammon boards. In the basement, gamers sit hunched over several computers, smoking joints and killing Orcs. It's a pretty funky place. Open: mon-sat 10-20. (Map area B5)

**Dutch Flowers** - *Singel 387, 624-7624*
*http://www.xs4all.nl/~dutchflw*

The beautiful canal on one side and an interesting, busy little street on the other make this a nice spot to take a break. There's a stack of magazines and comics, and good music on the stereo. It's located right in the centre of the city by Spui Circle. Their selection of weed and hash is also available in small amounts. *And* they serve beer. Open: sun-thurs 10-1; fri/sat 'til 2. (Map area C6)

**The T-Boat** - *Oude Schans 143*

A coffeeshop on a houseboat. That's pretty cool! I don't buy buds here or hang out inside, but in the summer, on a sunny day, it's fantastic: smoking on the big deck by the water, sipping a juice, getting a tan, watching the ducks and boats cruise by. Located between Nieuwmarkt and Waterlooplein. Open: daily (in summer)10-24. (Map area E5)

**The Otherside** - *Reguliersdwarsstraat 6, 421-1014*

As it's located right in the heart of the gay ghetto, it's mostly men that come here, but women are also welcome. It's a friendly spot and it's easy to meet people. The main drawback is the loud dance music. I think there's another gay coffeeshop called Downtown further along this street, too. Open: daily 11-1. (Map area D6)

**Tweedy** - *Vondelstraat 104, 618-0344*
*http://www.tweedy.nl*

Tweedy sits at the edge of Vondelpark just across the street from the Vondel Church. The people who work there aren't overly friendly, but they're not rude either, and I find it a pleasant place to get stoned. I especially like sitting at the back in one of the three train compartments, complete with overhead luggage racks full of magazines and backgammon sets. They also have cheap (*f*1) pool, and a good selection of candy bars. Open: daily 14-22 (longer in the summer). (Map area A7)

**Kashmir Lounge** - *Jan Pieter Heijestraat 85-87, 683-2268*

This whole place is adorned with Indian metal-work lampshades, embroidered fabrics, and coloured-glass candle holders. One incense-laden room is furnished with patterned carpets, pillows decorated with mirrors, and low wooden tables. And, as a reminder of where you really are, there's also a pinball machine, fusball, and a pool table. They have a small terrace out front in the summer, too. Open: mon-thurs 10-1; fri/sat 10-3; sun 11-1.

**Museum Coffeeshop** - *Oude Doelenstraat 20, 623-5267*

The owners of the Hash Marijuana Hemp Museum (just a few doors away) have done a nice job fixing up this place. There are lots of hemp decorations and some trippy murals. The corner location and big windows make it a great spot for watching all the sleazy action on the street. Upstairs is a beautiful, North African style chill-space, but it's not always open so you should ask before you head up. Open: daily 10-1. (Map area E5)

# SEEDS / GROW SHOPS

There are several reputable places to buy seeds around town, but over the past couple of years a lot of fly-by-night companies have also appeared selling inferior products. The reputable companies have spent years developing their strains in order to produce a stable, reliable seed. I've listed a few of them below. Remember that while it's legal to buy cannabis seeds in the Netherlands, it's illegal to import them into most other countries. You've been warned.

**Sagarmatha Seeds and Psychedelic Gallery** - *Marnixstraat 255, 638-4334*
*http://www.xs4all.nl/~seeds*

This company's motto, "highest on earth", refers in part to their name. Sagarmatha is what they call Mt. Everest in Nepal. The 100% organically produced seeds sold here aren't super cheap, but they're aimed at connoisseurs, who will appreciate the end result. They sell some very tasty strains including Bubbleberry, Mangolian Indica, and the particularly pleasurable Yumbolt. Check their web site for news, images of resin-coated plants, and some interesting links (see also 'Shrooms, Shopping chapter). Open: thurs-tues 12-17. (Map area B4)

**Sensi Seeds** - *Oudezijds Achterburgwal 150, 624-0386*
*http://www.sensiseeds.com*

The people who brought you the Hash Marijuana Hemp Museum run this business, too. You'll find everything you need for growing on sale here, starting with seeds. Like Sagarmatha, the seed prices are a bit high, but they have proven genetic quality and that attracts a lot of professional growers. They're always big winners at the Cannabis Cup and Highlife awards (see Festivals, Music chapter). It's worth stopping in here just to pick up their colour catalogue full of photos of beautiful buds. They also have a small shop near Central Station, at Nieuwendijk 26. Open: mon-sat 11-21; sun 11-18. (Map area E5)

### The Seed Bank - *Prins Hendrikkade 87, 777-2767*

Amsterdam's newest seed company is also it's oldest. Neville, whose potent strains earned him the respect of growers the world over when he started The Seed Bank in 1984, is back in business. From its home at The Emerald Triangle Trading Company (see Misc, Shopping Chapter) all his strains, developed from the original mother and father plants, are being sold again. Open daily 10-21. (Map area E4)

### After The Harvest - *Cornelis Troostraat 37, 470-8889*
*http://www.Amsterdampage.com*

This inviting shop caters to all your post-harvest needs. They sell the amazing Pollinator (for making hash), seed sorters, and even a machine called The Clipper that automatically manicures your buds! This is definitely the only store of its kind that I've ever heard of. In the back you'll find the Botanic Herbalist (see Misc, Shopping chapter), and a couple of doors down is a grow shop called Positive Grow. After The Harvest is open mon-sat 11-19:00.

### Hemp Works - *Nieuwendijk 13, 421-1762*
*http://www.xs4all.nl/~hemp*

Hemp Works sells a huge assortment of seeds: Sagarmatha Seeds, Sensi Seeds, and their in-house line - T.H.Seeds (which includes the incredible S.A.G.E. strain, which you may have tried at Katsu coffeeshop). Make your purchase during their 4:20 happy hour and get 10% off. That's also when you're most likely to find their resident seed expert, Adam, in the house. He knows a fuck of a lot about growing and is happy to share his knowledge. Open: daily 12-19. (Map area D3)

### The Flying Dutchman - *Oudezijds Achterburgwal 131, 428-4023*

This company sells their seeds from their shop of the same name, which is located in the Red Light District, just across the canal from the Cannabis College (see below). Choose from their own line, or from one of the other companies' products that are also available here. Open: daily 11-19. (Map area E5)

### Bio-B - *Bilderdijkstraat 194, 612-4009*

I don't know too much about these people, but I do know that they sell grow equipment at cheap prices. I think they also wholesale to other shops around town. Unfortunately, the last time I went in they weren't very helpful and they were playing a Cranberries tape - two strikes against them. Open: mon-sat 10-17. (Map area A5)

### Interpolm Amsterdam - *Prins Hendrikkade 11, 627-7750*
*http://www.interpolm.nl*

These guys are very conveniently located just across from Central Station. They renovated their shop recently and in addition to the grow equipment showroom, they have a little café, too (keep your eyes open for their coupons for a free cup of coffee). Open: mon 13-18; tues-fri 10-18; sat 10-17. (Map area E3)

### De Groeiwinkel - *Javastraat 74, 663-6378*

New and used growing supplies are sold here, as are seeds and a particularly nice soil mix. If you make the trek out east where this shop is located, think about visiting the Ij Brewery, the Troppenmuseum, and the Dapper Market as they're all in the same area (see the relevant chapters for details). Open: mon-sat 11-19. (Map area F7)

# HEMP STORES

**Hemp Works** - *Nieuwendijk 13, 421-1762*
*http://www.xs4all.nl/~hemp*

"Industrial Organic Wear". This is the designer hemp store in Amsterdam. Most of what they carry, like the 100% hemp baseball shirts, are on their own label. Other hemp clothes include jeans, dresses and lingerie, all displayed against a backdrop of hemp walls! They also sell hand blown glass pipes (check out the dragons and snakes), and they take custom orders if you have a design in mind. At the lounge in the back of the shop, deejays spin hip-hop and drum & bass. Open: daily 12-19. (Map area D3)

**Green Lands Hemp Store** - *Utrechtsestraat 26, 625-1100*

Jeans, jackets, shirts, hats and other clothing... made from hemp. Shampoo, soap, lotions... made from hemp. Writing paper, envelopes, edibles, everything in this store... made from hemp. Do yourself and this old planet a favour and find out more about this amazing plant and it's myriad of uses. Open: mon 13-18; tues-sat 11-18. (Map area E7)

# SHOPPING

Saturdays, at 17:00 or 18:00, most stores in Amsterdam lock their doors and they don't open again until Monday afternoon. However, many stores in "tourist areas" are now allowed to open on Sunday. Most stores stay open on Thursday nights until 21:00.

## MARKETS

### Albert Cuyp Markt - *Albert Cuypstraat (btwn Ferdinand Bolstr. & Van Woustr.)*

It's big and it's great! Amsterdam's most famous market is crowded with stalls and shoppers. You'll find everything here, from fruits and veggies, to clothes and hardware. Underwear is a good deal and so are plain cotton t-shirts (if yours are getting smelly). Just remember that you don't pick your own fruit and some of the vendors are assholes and will routinely slip a few rotten pieces into each bag. This happens to tourists and Dutch shoppers alike, so don't take it personally and don't be afraid to complain. To pick your own produce, shop at the Turkish stores that are found around most markets. Open: mon-sat 9-16. (Map area E8)

### Organic Farmers' Market - *Noordermarkt*

Its location at the foot of the Noorderkerk (North Church) lends a medieval feel to this fantastic organic market. All the booths sell healthy produce and products. Consequently, it's not really cheap, but if you like markets it's well worth a visit. Right around the corner, on the same day, is the Lindengracht market (see below). Another organic market (that also takes place on Saturdays) can be found at Nieuwmarkt from 9-16:00. The Noordermarkt is open Saturdays 9-16:00, too. (Map area C3)

### Lindenmarkt - *Lindengracht*

This is an all purpose market that's a bit more expensive than Albert Cuyp, but still has some good deals. It's in a beautiful neighbourhood and is right around the corner from the Organic Farmers' Market (see above). Open: sat 9-15. (Map area C3)

### Noordermarkt - *Noordermarkt*

For all you die-hard shoppers with nowhere else to go on Monday morning, this market's for you. There's both used and new clothes, books, records, and all kinds of junk. Great for bargain hunting. After it closes you can often find good stuff in the garbage. And for the record, there have been markets at this location since 1627! Open: mon 9-12. (Map area C3)

### Dappermarkt - *Dapperstraat*

A lot of immigrants from North Africa and the Middle East shop at this all purpose market, which is the cheapest in Amsterdam. There's also an Egyptian guy there who sells tasty falafels for just ƒ4. If you're staying at the Arena it's close - just across Oosterpark (see Parks, Hanging Out chapter). Open: mon-sat 9-16. (Map area H7)

### Ten Kate Market - *Ten Katestraat*

It's a bit out of the way for most tourists, but if you're in the area pay a visit to this lively neighbourhood market. I go there regularly to buy cheap popcorn from the

Turkish shops. Kinkerstraat, the main shopping street running by Ten Katestraat, lacks charm, but the streets behind the market are pretty. Open: mon-sat 9-17. (Map area A6)

**Waterlooplein Market** - *Waterlooplein*

This square is home to a terrific flea market where you can find clothes and jewellery and junk. Depending on where you're from, this can be a good place to buy a used leather jacket. It's easy to spend a couple of hours wandering around and, unlike other Amsterdam markets, you can try bargaining. Open: mon-sat 10-17. (Map area E6)

**De Rommelmarkt** - *Looiersgracht 38*

From the entrance, this flea market appears to be just a small storefront, but if you go in you'll find a sprawling 2 floors of old stuff. It's a lot of fun even if it's not the cheapest of markets. Mondays - mostly stamps, coins and cards. Tuesdays - mostly books, records, etc. Wednesdays - everything. Thursdays - second hand clothes. Fridays - closed. Saturdays - everything. Sundays - antiques. Open: 11-17. (Map area B6)

**Flower Market** - *Singel*

This pretty market is full of flowers and plants that are sold from barges on the Singel canal between Koningsplein and Muntplein. There are lots of good deals and it's probably the best place to buy tulip bulbs. Even if you're not interested in shopping here, it's a pretty market to wander through. Open: mon-sat 9-17. (Map area D6)

# BOOKS & MAGAZINES

### Kok Antiquariaat - *Oude Hoogstraat 14-18, 623-1191*

This is one of the best used bookstores in Amsterdam. It's spacious and well organized, with lots and lots of English titles. Make sure you look upstairs as well. Open: mon-fri 9:30-18; sat 9:30-17. (Map area D5)

### The American Book Center - *Kalverstraat 185, 625-5537*
*http://www.abc.nl*

I think this is the cheapest store for new books, especially for students, who get a 10% discount. They are the largest source of English language books in Europe! Look for bargain books in the basement. A few times a year they clear out all the old magazines and you can find stuff like *Hemp Times* for ƒ2.50. The Kalverstraat is one of the main pedestrian shopping streets in the city. Open: mon-sat 10-20 (thurs 'til 22); sun 11-18. (Map area D5)

### The Book Exchange - *Kloveniersburgwal 58, 626-6266*

Everything is very well-organized in this clean shop (there's none of that mustiness associated with so many used book stores) and you're bound to find something of interest. They have a big travel section with both guides and literature, and there's a German and French section, too. If you have some books to sell, I find that they pay the fairest price in town. Open: mon-fri 10-18; sat 10-17:30; sun 11:30-16. (Map area E5)

**Van Gennep** - *Nieuwezijds Voorburgwal 330, 626-4448*

A fantastic "remainder" bookstore. They have an impressive collection of quality English books, and prices start as low as ƒ4. Great for bargain hunting. Near Spui Circle. Open: mon 11-18; tues-fri 10-18 (thurs 'til 21:00); sat 11-18. (Map area D5)

**Vrolijk** - *Paleisstraat 135, 623-5142*

This shop advertises itself as "the largest gay and lesbian bookstore on the continent". It's located just off the Dam Square and it's usually pretty busy. If you're looking for something in particular, the staff are friendly and helpful. Open: mon 11-18; tues-fri 10-18 (thurs 'til 21); sat 10-17. (Map area D5)

**Vrouwen in Druk** - *Westermarkt 5, 624-5003*

A small, women's bookstore across from the beautiful, old Westerkerk and the Homomonument. Mostly used books as well as magazines and postcards. Open: mon-fri 11-18; sat 11-17. (Map area C4)

**Antiquariaat Lorelei** - *Prinsengracht 495, 623-4308*

Used books by and about women. Located in a little, cosy, canal-front shop. Open: wed-sat 12-18. (Map area C5)

**Intermale** - *Spuistraat 251, 625 0009*

This is a gay bookstore. It's a nice space with a good selection of books, magazines and some videos. They have gay guides to countries all around the world and a small porno section in the back. Open: mon 11-18; tues-sat 10-18; (thurs 'til 21). (Map area C5)

**J. de Slegte Boekhandel** - *Kalverstraat 48-52, 622-5933*

Some good deals on remainders can be found at this big store on the Kalverstraat. It lacks the charm of KOK (see above), but upstairs you'll find a huge selection of used books, many in English. Open: mon 11-18; tues-fri 9:30-18 (thurs 'til 21); sat 9:30-18; sun 12-17. (Map area D5)

**Gallerie Lambiek** - *Kerkstraat 78, 626-7543,*
*http://www.xxlink.nl/lambiek*

This is the most famous comic store in Amsterdam. They've got new, used and fanzines too. It's interesting to look over all the European comics and they've got lots of Canadian and American stuff as well. Collectors of "action figures" might also want to check out Henk Lie Comics & Manga Store (Zeedijk 136), and Vandal Com-X (Rozengracht 31). Lambiek is open: mon-fri 11- 18; sat 11-17; sun 13-17. (Map area C7)

**Evenaar** - *Singel 348, 624-6289*
*http://www.etrade.nl/evenaarreisboeken*

This travel bookshop has a fascinating collection. Works are organized by region and include not only guides and journals, but novels, political analyses and history - many by lesser known authors. Worth visiting for a browse if you're travelling onward from Holland. Open: mon-fri 12-18; sat 11-17. (Map area C5)

**Athenaeum Nieuwscentrum** - *Spui 14-16, 624-2972*
*http://www.athenaeum.nl*

For cheap magazines, check the bargain bin at this news shop on Spui Circle. I buy old *NME's* here for ƒ.50 and other music mags in the ƒ1-4 range. For new magazines and international papers, this is one of the best stores in Amsterdam. The sister bookstore next door is excellent, but not cheap. Open: mon-sat 8-21; sun 10-18. (Map area D5)

**Book Traffic** - *Leliegracht 50, 620-4690*

The owner of this used bookshop's got lots of English books and, sometimes, a bargain bin out front. There are a few other used bookshops located on this beautiful canal, too. Open: mon-fri 10-18; sat 11-18; sun 13-18. (Map area C4)

**Het Fort Van Sjakoo** - *Jodenbreestraat 24, 625-8979*
*http://www.xs4all.nl/~sjakoo*

"Specializes in Libertarian and radical ideas from the first to the fifth world and beyond". In addition to political books from around the world, this volunteer-run shop has a whole wall of fanzines and magazines, including lots of info on squatting. They've got cards, stickers, and shirts, too. Definitely worth a visit. Open: mon-fri 11-18; sat 11-17. (Map area E6)

**Cultural** - *Gashuismolensteeg 4*

The nice old guy who owns this hole-in-the wall has a few shelves of English paperbacks and a few piles of Life and other magazines from the '50s and '60s. It's not far from Dam square in a pretty area, so you might pass it while wandering about, but I forgot to check the opening hours. Sorry. (Map area C5)

**Oudemanhuis Boekenmarkt** - *Oudemanhuispoort*

This little book market is located in the neighbourhood of the university, in a covered alleyway that runs between Oudezijds Achterburgwal and Kloveniersburgwal. Used books and magazines in several languages are spread out on tables and stands. There are also maps, cards and, occasionally, funny pornographic etchings from centuries past for ƒ1-2. Open: mon-sat 10-16. (Map area E5)

# RECORDS, TAPES & CDs

**Forever Changes** - *Bilderdijkstraat 148, 612-6378*

This is a well-stocked store full of new and used records and CDs. They have really interesting stuff in many areas: '60s, punk, blues, etc. And check out the singles boxes on the counter. There are also some fanzines. Open: mon 13-18; tues-fri 10-18; sat 10-17. (Map area A6)

**Boudisque** - *Haringpakkerssteeg 10-18, 623-2603*
*http://www.boudisque.nl*

This is one of Amsterdam's best music stores. They have a big selection and they know what's hot. Lots of pop, punk, metal and dance, as well as music from all around the world. Mostly CDs, but still some vinyl. Open: mon 12-18; tues-fri 10-18 (thurs 'til 21); sat 10-18; sun 12-18. (Map area E3)

**Concerto** - *Utrechtsestraat 54-60, 624-5467*
*http://www.netcetera.nl/jazzfacts/concerto*

New and used records, tapes and CDs in a pretty neighbourhood. Good prices on used stuff and lots of vinyl. Well worth checking out. Open: mon-sat 10-18 (thurs 'til 21); sun 12-18. (Map area E7)

**Get Records** - *Utrechtsestraat 105, 622-3441*

While they mostly carry CDs here, there's still some vinyl that's worth digging into. They have a very select, up-to-date collection of punk, indie, hip-hop, etc. Open: mon 12-18; tues-sat 10-18 (thurs 'til 21); sun 12-18. (Map area E7)

**Fat Beats** - *Singel 10 (basement), 423-0886*
*http://www.fatbeats.com*

Fat Beats is the store to check out if you're looking for the newest hip-hop on vinyl. Much of it is independent and underground - there's a lot of white label stuff here. You'll also find some r&b and funk. Deejays often hang out and spin a few tracks in the basement. Also for sale is a small selection of CDs, tapes, and clothing. Open: mon-sat 11-19 (thurs 'til 21); sun 12-18. (Map area D3)

**Staalplaat** - *Staalkade 6, 625-4176*
*http://www.staalplaat.com*

You'll find this store appropriately located in a stark, concrete basement not far from the Waterlooplein flea market (see Markets, this chapter). It stocks a huge selection of underground music: industrial, experimental, electronic, noise. They fill mail orders world-wide. This is also a good place to look for posters advertising underground parties. Open: mon-fri 11-18; sat 11-17. (Map area E6)

**Back Beat Records** - *Egelantiersstraat 19, 627-1657*

Jazz, soul, funk, pop, blues, r&b: there's a lot packed into this store's three levels. It's not cheap, but what a selection. It's also located in the Jordaan. Open: mon-fri 11-18; sat 10-17. (Map area C4)

**Record Palace** - *Weteringschans 33, 622-3904*

This is another good place for collectors: they have sections for most kinds of music. Check out the autographed record covers on the wall. It's located not far from the famous Paradiso (see Music chapter). Open: mon-fri 11-18; sat 11-17; sun 12-17. (Map area C7)

**Distortion Records** - *Westerstraat 72, 627-0004,*
*http://www.xs4all.nl/~distort*

They advertise "loads of noise, lo-fi, punk rock, and indie". Collectors, especially of vinyl, are going to love this place. The owners here are definitely on top of things, and they have a good selection of dance music now, too. They're located just up the street from the Noorderkerk. Open: tues-fri 11-18 (thurs 'til 21); sat 10-18. (Map area C3)

**Record Mania** - *Hazenstraat 29, 620-9912*

Vinyl rules at this little shop in the Jordaan. It's beautiful to see all the bins full of LPs and singles just waiting to be browsed through. They also have some ƒ1 and ƒ2.50 bins. Open: tues-sat 13-18. (Map area B5)

**Roots** - *Jonge Roelensteeg 6, 620-4470*

Reggae lovers take note: the hole-in-the-wall that houses this shop is full of Jamaican beats, from roots to ragga and beyond. Check the African section, too. They stock some vinyl, but most of the selection consists of CDs, including a lot of re-issues at very affordable prices. The owners are a great source of information about festivals in and around Amsterdam. Open: tues-sat 10:30-18 (thurs ('til 21); sun 12:30-18. (Map area D5)

**De Plaatboef** - *Rozengracht 40, 422-8777*

"The Record Thief" has several stores around Holland. The Amsterdam store is very popular. They sell new and used CDs and LPs. My friend scored a really hot Fela Kuti record here for cheap. Open: mon 12-18; tues-sat 10-18 (thurs 'til 21). (Map area B4)

**Groove Connection** - *St. Nicolaasstraat 41, 624-7234*

Apparently, this is a really popular place with deejays, who come to hear what's new and hot. I like it because it makes me feel stoned when I step inside. If you're into cool dance music (in other words, stuff that ain't shit), you should drop by. (You might also want to check Outland Records at Zeedijk 22). Open: mon 14-18; tues-sat 11-18 (thurs 'til 21); sun 14-18. (Map area D4)

**Werelds** - *Van Limburg Stirumplein 22, 688-5483*

All kinds of new and used records are available here, but I particularly like the music from different parts of the world. I've lucked into some good African music here. It's right next door to The Overkant (see Coffeeshops, Cannabis chapter). Open: tues-fri 12-18 (thurs 'til 21); sat 11-17. (Map area B2)

**Sound of the Fifties** - *Prinsengracht 669, 623-9745*

Funk, soul, jazz, r&b, gospel and more. Prices aren't super cheap, but there are some gems to be found here. New and used. Open: mon 13-18; tues-sat 11:30-18. (Map area C6)

**Nauta** - *Singel 87, 625-2345*

I wandered into this unassuming shop this winter and found some great records. They don't have too much stock on hand, but cool stuff keeps popping up. Check the books and magazines, too. Open: mon-fri 12-18; sat 12-17; sun 13-17. (Map area D4)

**Wentelwereld** - *1e Bloemdwarsstraat 13a, 622-2330*

I was riding through the Jordaan and my eye spotted the row of ƒ2,50 bins at this used record store. I came out with a copy of *The Runaways Live in Japan*. Open: tues-fri 12-18; sat 12-17:30. (Map area B4)

**Datzzit** - *Prinsengracht 306, 622-1195*

One of Amsterdam's newer record stores, this shop is full of collectables. And not just records. They also have books, posters, some old toys, and other stuff. Open: mon-sat 10-18; sun 12-18. (Map area C5)

**Independent Outlet** - *Vijzelstraat 77, 421-2096*
*http://www.outlet.nl*

Punk and hardcore central. Vinyl (of course), and CDs. (see Misc, this chapter). Open: tues-fri 11-19 (thurs 'til 21); sat 11-18; sun 13-18. (Map area D7)

# CLUB FASHIONS

Amsterdam's club fashion shops stock a wide variety of designer labels, both international and local. They're also all good places to find information on parties and raves.

**Clubwear-House** - *Herengracht 265, 622-8766*
*http://www.xs4all.nl/~cwh*

Come inside where it's always friendly and always trippy. You can listen to young deejays (who are encouraged to come by and show off their stuff) while you check out wild clothing by new designers as well as more familiar names. There's also a great selection of limited edition tapes by various deejays, used records, and all the flyers for all the best parties. Open: mon-fri 11:30-18:30 (thurs 'til 20); sat 12-18. (Map area C5)

**Housewives and Haircuts on Fire** - *Spuistraat 130, 422-1067*
*http://www.xs4all.nl/~housew*

If you want to prepare a bit before you hit Amsterdam's clubs, stop into this multidimensional shop. Browse through the clubwear for something new or dig through the used clothing and accessories. Then have one of the hairdressers in the back do something funky to your head. They also sell records here and have deejays playing them. It's a pretty chill place and it's right in the centre of town. Open: mon-sat 11-19 (thurs 'til 22); sun 12-18; and, in summer, fri 'til 22. (Map area D4)

**Diablo** - *Oudezijds Voorburgwal 242, 623-4506*

Lots of intriguing clothing and accessories await you in this dark, grungy store. You should be able to find something new and different. Open: mon-fri 10:30-18 (thurs 'til 21); sat 10-17. (Map area D5)

# BODY ART

**Eyegasm** - *Kerkstraat 113, 420-5841*

Check this out - Eyegasm is the only tattoo shop in Europe that is owned and operated exclusively by women. They specialize in one-off custom work and offer a refreshing alternative to the heavily male atmosphere of so many tattoo parlours. In addition to the tattooing, piercing is also offered in an adjoining studio, so you can continue with your body art adventure before heading upstairs to the Hair Police (see below) to get your hair freakified. Throw some deejays into the mix and an art gallery that doubles as a waiting area, and you've got one wickedly unique spot. Open: mon-fri 12-19 (thurs 'til 21); sat 11-18. (Map area C7)

**Hair Police** - *Kerkstraat 113, 420-5841*
*http://www.hairpolice.com*

Whether you're thinking about extensions, dreadlocks, weaves or braids, or just a haircut, you should do it while you're here. Since they opened, Hair Police have set the standard for funky hair in Amsterdam. They share their space with Eyegasm (see above) which makes for a memorable visit. Because their prices are reasonable you should probably try to make an appointment. Open: mon-fri 12-19 (thurs 'til 21); sat 11-18. (Map area C7)

**Hanky Panky Tattooing** - *Oudezijds Voorburgwal 141, 627-4848*

You'll find that the international staff at Hanky Panky are very knowledgeable about their art. The selection of designs is immense, and of course you're welcome to bring in your own. Lots of famous rock stars have come through here. Go early to make an appointment. Be patient. There are also books and postcards available. Located in the Red Light District. Open: mon-wed 11-18; thurs-sat 11-20; sun 12-18 - longer hours in the summer. (Map area E5)

**Body Manipulations** - *Oude Hoogstraat 31, 420-8085*
*http://www.channels.nl/bodyman.html*

Along with tattoos, piercing is probably the most popular form of body art. They used to offer scarification and branding here, but now it's just piercing. The people who run the studio are more than happy to talk to you about the procedure and what pain (if any), is involved. They also have an excellent collection of books and magazines on the subject. Prices start at ƒ15 for an ear piercing (including stud), and ƒ30 for cartilage. Lip or eyebrow costs ƒ50. And tongue, nipple, navel, clit, penis, etc, start at ƒ50 (excluding jewellery). Open: mon-wed 12-18; thurs-sat 12-19. (Map area E5)

**Purple Circle** - *Geelvinckssteeg 10, 620-7661*

There's a Purple Circle in LA and now there's one here, too. The scissor-happy stylists at this cool studio operate out of a hole-in-the-wall near the Flower Market. They specialize in the same sort of stuff as the Hair Police gang. Open: mon-sat 12-19 (thurs 'til 21) (Map area D6)

# SMART SHOPS & 'SHROOM VENDORS

Surprise! You can buy magic mushrooms over the counter at several shops around town. Since the Dutch Ministry of Health has not found them to be hazardous when used responsibly, the government has decided to tolerate the sale of these little buggers in an open (hence, safe) manner. If you haven't tripped before make sure to consult with the person who's selling them first. They'll tell you how to take them and what to expect.

'Shrooms are also sold at "smart shops". These shops specialize in legal, mostly herbal, mind- and mood-enhancers of various sorts: stimulants, aphrodisiacs, relaxants, and hallucinogens. Smart shops have sprung up all around town over the last couple of years. Here a few of the more established and reputable ones.

**Kokopelli** - *Warmoesstraat 12, 421-7000*

Opened by the Conscious Dreams crew (see below), this is one of the hippest smart shops in Amsterdam. The space is beautiful - with a very mellow area at the back where you can drink a tea, surf the Net, listen to deejays, and enjoy the beautiful view over the water. The staff are tourist-friendly so feel free to ask for info on herbal ecstasy, mushrooms, smart drugs, or any of the other products on offer. There's talk of turning the basement into a living-room-like chill space for meditation and Ayahuasca sessions. It's located very close to Central Station. Open: daily 11-22. (Map area E4)

### Conscious Dreams - *Kerkstraat 117, 626-6907*
*http://www.consciousdreams.nl*

This was the first smart shop in the world! They pioneered the concept and it's always worth dropping into this gallery/shop to see what's new. In the back you'll find a large selection of smart drinks and drugs. They have all kinds, some that you might not know about, and they're happy to advise and inform you about their different uses. They also have lots of flyers for parties. It's a very trippy place. Come in... and be experienced. Open: mon-wed 11-19; thurs-sat 11-20; sun (in summer) 14-17. (Map area C7)

### The Botanic Herbalist - *Cornelis Trooststraat 37, 470-0889,*
*http://www.Amsterdampage.com*

A very cool store. This space, which they share with After the Harvest (see Seed/Grow Shops, Cannabis chapter) has, among other things, an extensive line of hemp products, including hemp snowboards! It is also a centre for people interested in psychoactive plants. Many are for sale, like the rare Salvia, and the staff at this laid-back shop know all about them and their uses. Or for something completely different, try the chocolate milk mix (containing a gram of weed), or their cannabis vegetable soup. Open: mon-sat 11-19:00.

### Chills & Thrills - *Nieuwendijk 17, 638-0015*
*http://www.chillsandthrills.com*

This smart shop has an amazing number of new and interesting products. This was the first place that I saw the mini vapourizer (a very healthy way to smoke cannabis). They also sell mushrooms, flavoured cannabis tea (1 gram in each bag), and cannabis chip dip mixes! Books, and magazines like *Weed World*, can be purchased here as well, and they have a record shop in the back. Open: mon-sat 11-21 (in summer 'til 22); sun 12-21. (Map area D3)

### The Headshop - *Kloveniersburgwal 39, 624-9061*

Mushrooms and spores are sold at competitive prices at this cool shop. It's conveniently located in the centre (see Misc, below). Open: mon-sat 11-18. (Map area E5)

### Sagarmatha Seeds and Psychedelic Gallery - *Marnixstraat 255, 638-4334*
*http://www.xs4all.nl/~seeds*

This shop, located in a cosy old storefront (see Seeds, Cannabis chapter), stocks the widest variety of mushrooms in Amsterdam. And the most potent, too. They even sell the fabled Philosophers' Stones. Stop in for experienced advice. And while you're there, check out the unique Grateful Dead batiks. Open: thurs-tues 12-17. (Map area B4)

# MISCELLANEOUS

### The Headshop - *Kloveniersburgwal 39, 624-9061*

Most, if not all, your drug paraphernalia needs can be met in the shops on the streets heading east off Dam square past the Grand Hotel Krasnapolsky (which, by the way, has very nice, clean toilets upstairs to the left off the lobby). I think the best store is The Headshop, which has been in business since 1968. Lots and lots of pipes, bongs and papers; plus books, magazines, postcards, stickers and the required collection of incense and Indian clothing. They also sell magic mushrooms and spores for growing your own. They have a good reputation and sometimes it gets very crowded. Just across the street (Nieuwe Hoogstraat 3) the same owners have another shop called Oriëntal Fantasies. The Headshop is open: mon-sat 11-18. (Map area E5)

## Independent Outlet - *Vijzelstraat 77, 421-2096*
*http://www.outlet.nl*

IO is a way cool store selling punk and hardcore records, skateboards and clothing, and hard to find fanzines and magazines. The records and CDs have their own home in the back where you can also grab a coffee and rest your dogs in the 50's style diner booths. And the stylin' clothes on offer are really cheap for Northern Europe. This is also a good place to find out about skate events and where punk and hardcore bands are playing. Open: tues-fri 11-19 (thurs 'til 21); sat 11-18; sun 13-18. (Map area D7)

## Kelere Kelder - *Prinsengracht 285*

*Kelere* is Amsterdam slang for clothes, and *kelder* means cellar. Not surprisingly then, you'll find this used clothes store in the cellar of a long-standing squat on the Prinsengracht. It's cooperatively-run and, except for some new political t-shirts with unique designs, almost everything else in the store is used. There are racks of clothes, some books and fanzines, records, other odds and ends, and even a big *f*1 basket! Prices are very cheap, so you probably won't come away empty-handed. Usually open: fri-sun 13-18. (Map area C4)

## The Emerald Triangle Trading Company - *Prins Hendrikkade 87, 777-2767*

Located in an old house right across the street from Central Station, this tiny new store will be selling all sorts of custom made artwork. When they open this spring they'll have shirts, posters, pipes, music and books, and lots of Grateful Dead stuff. This is also the home of The Seed Bank (see Seed/Grow Shops, Cannabis chapter). Pop in when you're doing your present shopping. Open daily 10-21. (Map area E3)

## Aboriginal Art and Instruments - *Spuistraat 183b, 423-1333*
*http://www.xs4all.nl/~aai*

This is the only store of it's kind in Europe, so it's no surprise that I'd never seen such beautiful didjeridoos until I wandered into this shop/gallery. The owner travels to the outback in Australia and hand-picks these unique instruments himself to make sure that he gets only the highest quality. Also for sale are CDs and other Aboriginal artwork. If you already have a didjeridoo, stop by for info about jam sessions. Open: tues-sat 12-18; sun 14-18. (Map area D5)

## 3-D Holograms - *Grimburgwal 2, 624-7225*

This shop is almost like a hologram museum. There are some great works of art here and a good selection of hologram jewellery, stickers, cards, etc. You might want to take a look if you have to buy some presents for all those loved ones back home. There's also a good pancake place upstairs (see Restaurants, Food chapter). If you're really into holograms, check out the big white sculpture on the grass just over the bridge beside the American Hotel (Leidseplein): it's full of holographic rainbow prisms. Open: mon 13-17:30; tues-fri 12-18; sat 12-17:30; sun 13-17:30. (Map area D5)

## Day* 1 - *Nieuwe Nieuwstraat 27C - 423-6822*

These guys are nestled upstairs above a record shop called Soul Food (that was playing some pretty chunky beats last time I was there). They sell a select line of street wear that includes their own line, magazines like the Beastie Boys' *Grand Royal*, skate stuff and as their flyer says "whatever". They also have an iMac that you can use for surfing (f5 for 30 minutes). Open: mon 13-19; tues-sat 11-19 (thurs 'til 21); sun 14-18. (Map area D4)

### Humana - *Gravenstraat 22, 623-3214*

If you like shopping for used clothes, stop by this store. It's really hit and miss. Sometimes they have only shit, but I've also found some fantastic deals on all kinds of stuff: perfect Levis for f18, a leather jacket for f35, and once they had a big rummage sale and I bought a TV for f12! The money goes to third world development projects. They also accept donations, if you want to lighten your pack a bit. Open: mon 13-18; tues-fri 9:30-18 (thurs 'til 21); sat 9:30-17; sun 12-17. (Map area D4)

### The Fair Trade Shop - *Heiligeweg 45, 625-2245*

Crafts, clothes and jewelry from developing countries. Also, fair-trade coffee, tea, chocolate, nuts and wine. Lots of unusual gift ideas. It's not the cheapest store, but there are some deals, and the money is going back to the right people. Open: mon 13-18; tues-fri 10-18 (thurs 'til 21), sat 10-17:30; sun 12-17. (Map area D6)

### The Old Man - *Damstraat 16, 627-0043*

This is a drug paraphernalia shop with a wide choice of pipes. Up one set of stairs you'll come upon a baffling array of weapons and lots of posters of chicks with guns. Some of you might be more comfortable up the other stairs where they sell snowboards, skateboards, and inline skates. Open: mon 10-18; tues-sat 9-18 (thurs 'til 21); sun 10:30-18. Hours are sometimes extended in summer. (Map area D5)

### Cash Converters - *Amstelveenseweg 39, 685-0500*

If you like collecting junk, swing by this second-hand store at the far end of Vondelpark. Some things are ridiculously overpriced, but other stuff is a steal. I bought a really nice turntable here for next to nothing. And I got a hot air popcorn popper. My friend found a Funkadelic CD for f10. Anyway, don't go out of your way, but if you decide to sell your walkman or you're looking for something specific, it could be worth a visit. You can bargain here, too. Open: mon 13-18; tues-fri 10-18 (thurs 'til 21); sat 10-17.

### Donalds E Jongelans - *Noorderkerkstraat 18, 624-6888*

You know when you walk into an old-style corner store and find a great pair of sunglasses in a dusty display case? That's what this store feels like, except it's not dusty. They have a fantastic selection of old (but not used) sunglasses and frames at reasonable prices. It's right behind the Noorderkerk, so you might want to stop in if your at either of the markets held here (see Markets, above). Open: mon-sat 11-18. (Map area C3)

### China Town Liquor Store - *Geldersekade 94-96, 624-5229*

For some reason I think that this liquor store is cheaper than others, but I don't know if it's true. Anyway, this sleazy strip is where I buy my booze and a couple of doors down is a great Chinese supermarket, Wah Nam Hong. There's a slick new liquor store in the basement of the Albert Heijn on Nieuwezijds Voorburgwal (see Supermarkets, Food chapter) that's open longer hours. The China Town Liquor Store is open: mon-sat 9-18. (Map area E4)

### De Witte Tandenwinkel - *Runstraat 5, 623-3443*

I love the window of this store. They have the world's largest collection of tooth-brushes! All shapes, all sizes and styles. They make unusual gifts, and they don't weigh much - which is a bonus when you're travelling. Take a look if you're in the neighbourhood. Open: mon 13- 18; tues-fri 10-18; sat 10-17. (Map area C5)

### Studio Spui - *Spui 4, 623-6926*

Check this shop for good specials on film close to its expiry date. Open: mon 10:30-18; tues-fri 09:30-18 (thurs 'til 21); sat 10-17:30. (Map area D5)

### Photo Processing - Kruidvat - *Kalverstraat 187*

This is the cheapest place I know to get photos processed in Amsterdam. It takes two days and I had a roll of 24 colour prints done for ƒ10. Just a bit more expensive is the Dirk van den Broek supermarket at Heinekenplein. Photo booths, to have pass-port sized photos taken (ƒ6-7), can be found at the main post office (Singel 250), and at Central Station. (Map area D5)

### Kinko's Copy Center - *Overtoom 62, 589-0910*

I'm not crazy about this joint because I had some work done here and they didn't do a good job. But they're open 24 hours a day, 7 days a week, so if you need to send a fax you can do it after 20:00, when phone rates are cheaper. (Map area A7)

### Postcards

If you don't care whether Amsterdam is pictured on the ones you send home, look for the Boomerang *free* postcard racks. You'll find them in movie theatre lobbies, cafés and bars all around town.

# HANGING OUT

This is the chapter for people who enjoy just wandering about the streets, seeing who's around, listening to music in the park, and for those of you who are really broke. During the warm months the streets and parks of Amsterdam come alive and you don't need a lot of money to find entertainment. I've also got a couple of suggestions for when it's rainy or cold.

## PARKS

Amsterdam has many beautiful parks that are well used throughout the year, but particularly in the summer months when the sunset lingers for hours and the sky stays light 'til late. Picnics are a very popular in Holland - you can invite all your friends at once, instead of just the small number that would otherwise fit in your apartment. After dark, however, it's best not to hang out in any of these parks alone.

### Vondelpark
*http://www.dds.nll~park (a Dutch site, but with lots of nice photos)*

When the weather is warm this is the most happening place in the city. Crowds of people stroll through the park enjoying the sunshine and the circus-like atmosphere. Walk along the main pathways and notice the tarot and palm readers sitting peacefully in the shade of the trees. And all the jugglers practising with plates and balls and bowling pins, who look like jesters from a medieval court (especially if you've just had a smoke). Wander further into the park past old men fishing in quiet ponds and into the rose garden for an olfactory overload. Come out on the other side by a large field of cows and goats and even a couple of llamas! It's easy to forget you're in a city. About now you may want to look for one of the cafés in the park in order to buy an ice cream. Then listen to some music being performed in the band-shell, or to one of the dozens of musicians and bands jamming throughout the park. Look at the bright coloured parrots (I'm not kidding) in the trees. Play some footbag or frisbee. Watch the break-dancers. Or maybe you just want to join all the other people laying half-dressed on the grass, reading, smoking, playing chess, or just sleeping. Trams 1, 2, 5, 6, 20. (Map area A8)

### Amsterdamse Bos (Woods)

It's a bit of a trek to get out to this big patch of green, but what a gorgeous place. There are lots of winding bike and hiking paths, waterways, a gay cruising area, and some wild parties when the weather is nice. In an large tent along the west side of the Nieuwe Meer (New Lake) is a cool café called Club Animeer. They're open in the summer and serve drinks and snacks and, sometimes, sushi dinners. They have parties there, too. In another part of the Bos is a big field where you can lie on your back and jets from nearby Schiphol fly really low right over you: not exactly peaceful, but I enjoy it! Free maps and information are available from the Bosmuseum (on Koenenkade at the end of Bosbaan; open daily 10-17; 643-1414). Bus 170, 171, 172.

### Oosterpark (East Park)

Lots of ducks and lots of toddlers waddle around this park that's full of people strolling along the water and playing soccer in the big field. It also draws a lot of drummers (since that was banned in Vondelpark). The beautiful old band-shell is sometimes used for parties like the Oosterpark Festival in the first week of May, or the occasional reggae party. It's right by the Arena (see Places to Sleep), the Dappermarkt (see Markets, Shopping chapter), and the Tropenmuseum. Tram 9. (Map area G8)

### Sarphatipark

This pretty little park is really close to the Albert Cuyp Market (see Markets, Shopping chapter), and Katsu and YoYo (see Coffeeshops, Cannabis chapter). If you get the fixings for a picnic you can go here to pig out and smoke. Trams 24, 25.

### Wertheimpark

This small park is located on a canal just a block away from the Waterlooplein flea market (see Markets, Shopping chapter) and it's an ideal place to cool your heels and catch your breath after battling the crowds. It's peaceful under the big trees by the water. The Desmet theatre (see Film chapter) is just across the street. Tram 9. (Map area F6)

# PUBLIC GARDENS & SQUARES

### Gardens

The public gardens behind the Rijksmuseum are a pleasant, uncrowded place to sit and relax with a joint. The Stedelijk (modern art) Museum has a sculpture garden out back near Museumplein to which admission is free. Finally, you wouldn't really hang out in the Begijnhof, but it's a beautiful, old part of Amsterdam that should be seen. Look for an entrance behind the Amsterdam Historical Museum. There's also an entrance just off Spui Circle, through an arched doorway between Nieuwezijds Voorburgwal and the Esprit Café. Inside that entrance there's a plaque describing the interesting history of this pretty courtyard.

### Leidseplein

I mention this square in the music chapter as a place to catch street musicians. If the weather is good there are also sure to be street performers who sometimes line up for their chance to entertain the throngs of tourists (and make some dough). A lot of these artists are very talented and you can see their professionalism as they work the crowds between each unicycling, fire-eating, juggling trick, and how they deal with the inevitable disruptive drunk. If you do have a good time watching these people be sure to drop something in the hat. At the far end of the square, in front of the big movie theatre, are some cool, bronze lizard sculptures. And just across the street from there, carved high up on the marble pillars, is that age-old proverb "*Homo Sapiens Non Urinat In Ventum*", which is Latin for "don't piss in the wind".

### Museumplein

Some of Holland's most famous museums are situated around this giant square, hence the name. Two years of renovations are just being completed and, except for the underground parking garages, the plans look pretty nice. The skateboard ramps and basketball courts that gave so much character to the area will be back. There'll also be lots of park space and an ice rink in winter. (Map area C8)

### Dam Square

This huge, historic square in front of the palace is quiet in the winter, but there's almost always something going on in the summer. Unfortunately, there are a lot of pickpockets and other sleazy creeps around here. Keep your eyes open and don't buy drugs from any of the scummy dealers: you'll definitely get ripped off. (Map area D4)

# LIBRARIES

**Public Library** - *main branch Prinsengracht 587, 523-0900*
*http://www.oba.nl*

You have to be a member to borrow books, of course, but there's a lot to do here if you're not. If you ask at the information desk inside they'll give you English newspapers and magazines like *Time* and *Newsweek* to read. It's a good way to catch up on news if you've been travelling for awhile. They also have interesting photo exhibitions on the ground floor, and a couple of computer terminals with free Internet access. One terminal can be reserved by phone or in person for a maximum of 30 minutes. The other is "first come, first served". Note that there are no facilities for downloading or printing. In the cafeteria you'll find more newspapers and magazines from around the world, many in English. On the first floor there's a good selection of English novels and any other section in the library will also have a lot of English books and magazines. Comics are also on the first floor. The travel section on the third floor has shelves of books about Holland and any other country you might be heading to. On the top floor is a music section with lots of magazines, and their CD collection with listening facilities. Finally, if you're looking for a flat or need to sell something, the bulletin board in the front entrance is well used. The collection at this library is still pretty good, but over the past few years the building has become increasingly crowded, dirty and under-staffed. And now you have to pay to use the toilets too! Open: mon-13-21; tues-thurs 10-21; fri/sat 10-17; sun (oct-mar only) 13-17. (Map area C6)

**Netherlands Film Museum Library** - *Vondelstraat 69-71, 589-1400*

This library is part of the Netherlands Film Museum (see Film chapter) and lies right at the edge of Vondelpark. It's a bright, airy space, that's perfect for browsing in if you're a film-lover. A large percentage of their books are in English and there are plenty of magazines, too. You can't check books out, but there is a photocopier in the back. Check your bags in the lockers by the entrance - you get your guilder back when you leave. When you're finished, head up the street to the beautiful and cheap Manege Café (see Cafés). Open: tues-fri 10-17; sat 11-17. (Map area A8)

# SNOOKER & PING PONG

**De Keizers Snooker Club** - *Herengracht 256, 623-1586*

There's nowhere I know to play free snooker, but you can play here for ƒ10 an hour per table (no matter how many people are playing) and that's a pretty good deal. This price is valid daily 12-19. (Map area C5)

**Tafeltennis Centrum Amsterdam** - *Keizersgracht 209, 624-5780*

The free ping pong place in a squat that I wrote about in past editions is gone, so now it's pay to play again. This table tennis club charges ƒ14 an hour per table. They have a bar with food and drink, and the last time I was there they were playing old Rolling Stones. It's a neighbourhoody kind of place and there's often a table free, but to avoid disappointment you should probably call ahead to reserve. The entrance is a bit tricky to find. Walk down the hall, out the back door and across the courtyard. Open: mon-sat 13:30-1; sun 13-20. (Map area C5)

# FREE CONCERTS

**Het Concertgebouw** - *Concertgebouwplein 2, 671-8345*
*http://www.channels.nl/concertb.html*

Every Wednesday at 12:30 this famous concert hall, world-renowned for it's acoustics, throws opens its doors to the proletariat for a free half-hour performance. These concerts are extremely popular so whether it's in the main hall (2000 seats) or the smaller one (500 seats), you should get there early.

**Stopera Muziektheater** - *Waterlooplein 22, 625-5455*

Every Tuesday at 12:30 this modern concert hall, which is home to Amsterdam's ballet and opera, presents a free half-hour concert in its Boekman Zaal. It's also well-attended, so go early. Closed, however, in the summer months. (Map area E6)

**Vondelpark Bandshell** - *Vondelpark*

Free concerts are presented here in the summer (see Parks, this chapter). You'll find a schedule posted at the main entrance to the park. (Map area A8)

# VIRGIN MEGASTORE

**Magna Plaza** - *Nieuwezijds Voorburgwal 182, 622-8929*

The Magna Plaza is worth stepping into just to see the beautiful old building that used to house the main post office. Among all the upscale boutiques you'll find the Virgin Megastore. I come in from time to time to check out the 4 or 5 small screens with headphones showing videos like *Jerry Springer's Too Hot for TV*. There used to be more screens. Maybe they got tired of me standing there watching for two hours. Before you leave, stop by the book section and read a few of those magazines that are too expensive to buy. You can also purchase a can of Virgin Cola here for just ƒ1. Open: mon 11-18; tues-sat 9:30-18; sun 12-18. (Map area D4)

# SKATEBOARDING

The two ramps at Museumplein, where some of the skaters were doing mind-blowing things, will also be back after the renovations are complete. Down by the RAI convention centre (look on your map, it's a big building in the south end of Amsterdam), you'll also find skaters doing some good shit. There's also a big half-pipe under the highway bridge by Flevopark. Take tram 14 to the end of the line, walk through the underpass and turn right. Along with the pipe is some great graffiti. For more detailed info, stop in at Independent Outlet (see Shopping chapter), or Subliminal (Nieuwendijk 134, 428-2606) and they'll tell you what's up.

# KITE FLYING & JUGGLING

Because it's flat and windy, Holland is a great country for kite flying, especially at the beach. They make some pretty cool, compact ones these days and a growing number of people are actually travelling with kites. Try Joe's Vliegerwinkel (Nieuwe Hoogstraat 19, 625-0139). They sell all kinds of kites, and footbags, too! (Map area E5)

The Juggle Store (Kloveniersburgwal 54, 420-1980) is the place to find everything you need for juggling as well as info about juggling events around Holland and the rest of the world. They're open: tues-sat 12-17. (Map area E5)

# TOWER CLIMBING

Great views! Good exercise! Get off your ass!

Westerkerkstoren - *Westerkerk*. Open: apr-sept; mon-sat 10-16; ƒ3. The highest.
Zuiderkerkstoren - *Zuiderkerk*. Open: jun-sept; wed-sat 14-16; ƒ3.
Oudekerkstoren - *Oudekerk*. Open: jun-sept; wed-sat 14-16; ƒ3.
Beurs van Berlage - *Damrak 277*. Open: tues-sun 10-16; ƒ6.

**New Metropolis** - *Oosterdok 2, tel: 0900-919-1100*

I don't think this new science centre is worth the high admission price (see Museums), but if it's not too windy, the big public deck outside isn't a bad place to hang for a bit and look out over the city. Just climb the big steps out front, and remember to take some munchies. Unfortunately, most of the year they close before sunset. Open: sun-thurs 10-18:00 ('til 21:00 in July and August); fri/sat 10-21:00. (Map area F3)

# SAUNAS

**Sauna Fenomeen** - *1e Schinkelstraat 14, 671-6780*

In spite of the fact that it's in a squat (now legalized), this health club is clean, modern, and well-equipped. People of all ages, shapes and sizes come here. When you enter, give your name and get a locker key from the reception booth on the right. On the left is a changing room with instructions and rules in both English and Dutch. You can bring your own towel or rent one there for ƒ1.50. Then get naked, have a shower, and try out the big sauna or the Turkish steam bath! There is also a café serving fresh fruit, sandwiches, juices and teas. It's a relaxing place to unwind and read the paper or just listen to music and veg. Also available at extra charges are massages, tranquillity tanks, and tanning beds. Monday is for women only, and the rest of the week is mixed. Thursday, Saturday and Sunday are smoke-free. The price, if you're finished before 18:00, is ƒ10. After that it's ƒ12.50. It's located just past the western end of Vondelpark. Open: daily 13-23. Closed for two months in the summer.

**Marnixbad** - *Marnixplein 9, 625-4843*

This place is a lot closer to the centre. Sauna and shower ƒ12.75, or ƒ15.50 if you want to swim, too. Just a shower (without a sauna) costs ƒ3. Bring your own towel. Thursday is for women only. Open: tues-sun 10-16 and 19-22:30. (Map area B3)

# MUSEUMS

There are so many museums in this city that it could take you weeks to see them all. I'm only going to tell you about the lesser-known museums: ones that aren't in every tourist brochure. For basic information about the big ones, like the Rijksmuseum and the Van Gogh Museum, check the end of this chapter.

## THE UNUSUAL ONES

### The Sex Museum - *Damrak 18, 622-8376*

It's true that you could see almost everything here in the Red Light District for free, but admission is only ƒ4.50 and it's fun to tell your friends you went to the Sex Museum. The exhibits, which were getting pretty run down over the years, have been fixed up and the museum is looking a lot better. I particularly like the pornography from the turn of the century. One of the best parts of the museum is the two 7-foot-high penis chairs where you can pose for photos. Don't forget your camera! Open: daily 10-23:30. (Map area E4)

### The Erotic Museum - *Oudezijds Achterburgwal 54, 624-7303*

This collection is large (covers 5 floors) and varied, but unfortunately much of it is unlabelled. They have drawings by John Lennon, collages from Madonna's *Sex*, and a very ugly, very funny, pornotoon from Germany. You can also push a button that sets a dozen or so vibrators into action! There is a floor of hard-core videos and phone sex, and above that a rather tame S/M room. There's only one reference to gay male sex in the entire museum, however, a surprising omission considering Amsterdam's status as the gay capital of Europe. Admission ƒ5. Open: daily 11-1. (Map area E4)

### The Hash Marihuana Hemp Museum - *Oudezijds Achterburgwal 148, 623-5961*

The addition of the word "hemp" to this museum's name came after a major renovation and updating of the collection by Chris Conrad, author of the books *Hemp: Lifeline to the Future*, and *Hemp for Health*. At the entrance you'll find pamphlets and booklets on hemp and its uses, many of which are free. They also have books, magazines, and hemp products (including seeds) for sale. The exhibit consists of photos, documents, videos and artifacts dealing with all aspects of the amazing hemp plant including history, medicinal uses and cannabis culture. There's even a grow room. And if you're hungry for more info they also have a small reference library. Eagle Bill, the guy who really popularized the Vaporizer, is often in the back, demonstrating how it works. The vaporizer is a glass waterpipe that uses a powerful heat source to "vaporize" the THC-bearing resin without actually burning the weed in the bowl. It's a healthy alternative to filling your lungs with smoke, and it gets you wasted! He'll give you a free taste, but you should definitely make a small donation. Located in the Red Light District. Admission ƒ8. Open: daily 11-22. (Map area E5)

### Heineken Brewery - *Stadhouderskade 78, 523-9436*

This place was better when it was a working brewery and it only cost ƒ.50 to get in. Now the price is ƒ2 (which goes to UNICEF) for an explanation of Heineken history and the beer making process. Be sure to ask your guide about the kidnapping of Freddie Heineken! At the end of the tour you get what you really came for: a half hour of all the beer you can drink and a plate of cheezies. If it's your birthday you get a free mug. Tours are weekdays at 9:30 and 11. From June 1st to September 15th there are also tours at 13:00 and 14:30. And in July and August there are tours on Saturdays as well, at 11, 13 and 13:30. Tickets should be purchased in advance. Trams 16, 24, 25. (Map area D8)

### The Torture Museum - *Damrak 20-22, 639-2027*

Don't leave Amsterdam without visiting this unique collection of torture instruments. It's very educational. You'll learn where expressions like "putting the pressure on" originated. The museum is nicely laid out in an old house and lit with dingy, dungeon lighting. Each object has a small plaque explaining its function, and by and on whom it was inflicted. Detailed drawings illustrate their use. If you aren't already aware of Christianity's bloody history this is the place to see, quite graphically, just what has been done to people in the name of "god". (And speaking of god, what do you get when you cross an agnostic, an insomniac, and a dyslexic? Someone who stays up all night wondering if there's a dog.) Adults ƒ7.50; students ƒ5.50. Open: daily 10-23. (Map area E4)

### Tropenmuseum - *Linnaeusstraat 2, 568-8215*
*http://www.kit.nl/tropenmuseum*

This is one of the big ones that's in every guidebook. I'm including it here because it's such an amazing place, yet many visitors choose to skip it. This beautiful old building in eastern Amsterdam houses a fantastic collection of artifacts and exhibits from and about the developing world. The permanent exhibition uses model villages, music, slide shows, and lots of push-button, hands-on displays to give you a feel for everyday life in these countries. There are also changing exhibitions in the central hall and photo gallery. At the entrance you'll find listings for films and music in the adjoining Souterijn theatre (see Film chapter), but they're not included in the admission price. Adults ƒ10-12.50; students ƒ5-7.50. Open: mon-fri 10-17; sat/sun 12-17. (Map area H7)

### De Poezeboot (Cat Boat) - *a houseboat on the Singel opposite #20, 625-8794*

Attention cat lovers! This isn't really a museum, but what the fuck? Spend some time on this boat playing with dozens of love-hungry stray cats who now have a home thanks to donations from the public and volunteers who help out here. The boat is free to visit, but you're expected to make a contribution on your way out. Grab a postcard for your cat back home. Open: daily 13-16. (Map area D3)

### Tattoo Museum - *Oudezijds Achterburgwal 130, 625-1565*
*http://www.tattoomuseum.com*

Welcome to a very cool museum. The collection was assembled by the owner of Hanky Panky Tattooing (see Misc, Shopping chapter). It includes many photos from around the world, a mummified arm from Peru, and some tattooed skin from 1850. There's also a reference library (accessible by appointment). Special exhibitions are planned for the future, as are demonstrations by world famous tattoo artists. If you're thinking about getting one while you're in Amsterdam, visit this museum first for a little inspiration. Admission is ƒ5. Open: tues-sun 12-18 in summer; 12-17 in winter. (Map area E5)

### Electric Ladyland - The First Museum of Florescent Art
*2e Leliedwarsstraat 5, 420 3776*

It took 7 years to complete this small, very trippy, museum in the basement of this tiny shop, and when you see it you'll know why. It includes an intricate cave-like environment where you can push buttons that light up different areas of the space and play Jimi Hendrix. There are also display cases where minerals and fluorescent artifacts from all over the world are displayed under lights of different wavelengths, revealing startling, hidden colours. A ƒ5 donation gets you an informative booklet and access to the collection. Open afternoons Tuesday to Saturday or call for an appointment. (Map area B4)

### Woonboot Museum (Houseboat Museum) - *across from Prinsengr. 296, 427-0750*
*http://www.xs4all.nl/~houseboatmuseum*

The 84 year old ship housing this museum will show you what it's like to live on one of Amsterdam's approximately 2500 houseboats. There are also scale models of other boats, photos, a slide show, and displays intended to answer all those questions you have about life on the canals. Admission is ƒ3.75. Open: tues-sun 10-17. (Map area C5)

### Condom Museum - *Warmoesstraat 141, 627-4174*
*http://www.condomerie.com*

This tiny museum is made up of a colourful assortment of condom packages from around the world. The display is housed in a small glass case in the The Condomerie (see Sex Chapter). It doesn't take long to view the collection, but checking out the names and logos on the boxes (like the camoflage condom - "don't let them see you coming") is good for a laugh. Open: mon-sat 11-17. (Map area D4)

### Coffee and Tea Museum - *Warmoesstraat 67, 624-0683*

I didn't find the collection of coffee grinders and roasters terribly exciting, but it sure smelled great in the second floor of this coffee store. The business has been in the same family for five generations and in the same building for 140 years! Two nice old guys gave me a cup of joe and told me some stories about the good old colonial days. Open: tues/fri/sat 14-16:30. (Map area E4)

### The Smallest House In Amsterdam - *Singel 7*

The front of this house is only 1.01 metres wide! Property taxes were based on the width of the front of the house when this one was built, so they were pretty clever. You can't go inside, but it's still cool to take a look if you're walking by. It's not a museum. People live there. I used to know somebody who lived in the third smallest house in Amsterdam. She hated it when tourists would knock on her door to ask if they could look around the third littlest house in Amsterdam, so don't do it. There are other tiny houses around, including: Haarlemmerstraat 43 (1.28 metres wide); Oude Hoogstraat 22 (2.02 metres wide); Singel 166 (1.84 metres wide). (Map area D3)

### National Trade Union Museum (Vakbonds Museum) - *Henri Polaklaan 9, 624-1166*
*http://www.fnv.nl/~Vakbondsmuseum*

In the late 1800's, the famous architect Hendrik Berlage was commissioned to design the head office for the General Dutch Diamond Cutters Union. That union was the first in The Netherlands to win its workers the right to a vacation, and the first in the world to attain an eight-hour working day! The building is beautiful and it's fitting that it now houses this museum of the Dutch trade union movement. Most of the exhibits, which include displays about union activities of the past and present, are in Dutch, but a free English guide is available at the front desk. It kind of makes you want to get out your old, scratchy Woody Guthrie albums. Admission is ƒ5. Tram 9 to Plantage Kerklaan. Open: tues-fri 11-17; sat 13-17. (Map area F6)

**Eyeglass Museum (Brilmuseum)** - *Gasthuismolensteeg 7, 421-2414*

I thought this new museum sounded kind of interesting - a history of eyeglasses on display in an early 17th century house. But my curiosity wasn't strong enough to warrant the ƒ10 admission. Some of you 4-eyes might want to take a peek, though. Open: wed-sat 12-18. (Map area C5)

**Vrolijk Museum** - *Meibergdreef 15, 566-9111 (beeper 841)*

I haven't been here either, but listen to this: an 18th and 19th century collection of some professor and his son's embryological and anatomical specimens! Weird. It's out of the way in south-east Amsterdam and visits are by appointment only. Have a good time; I'm off to watch *Frankenhooker* again.

# THE BIG ONES

Here is some basic information on Amsterdam's biggest and most famous museums. They all have impressive collections and can get quite crowded during peak season. If you're here in the third week of April, ask the VVV about **Museum Weekend** - when all the big ones are free.

A **Museum Card** - good for one year - costs ƒ55 (ƒ25 if you're under 25!) and is available at most of these museums. It gets you in free or at a substantial discount to almost all the big ones in Holland. If you're planning to go to more than a few of these, are visiting other cities in The Netherlands, or are returning within a year, then it's a good deal. You need one photo.

*Under the Rijksmuseum.*

**Rijksmuseum** -
*Stadhouderskade 42, 674-7000*
Home to 20 Rembrandts. Open: daily 10-17. ƒ15; 18 and under ƒ7.50.
Trams 2, 5, 6, 7, 10, 20. (Map area C8)

**Vincent van Gogh Museum** - *Paulus Potterstraat 7 570-5200*
Open: daily 10-18. ƒ12.50; 17 and under ƒ5. Trams 2, 3, 5, 12, 20. (Map area B8)

**Anne Frank House** - *Prinsengracht 263, 556-7100*
Open: daily 9-19. ƒ10; 17 and under ƒ5. Trams 13, 14, 17, 20. (Map area C4)

**Stedelijk Museum** - *Paulus Potterstraat 13, 573-2737*
*http://www.stedelijk.nl*
Modern art. Open: daily 11-17. ƒ9; 16 and under ƒ4.50. Trams 2, 3, 5, 12, 16. (Map area B8)

**Rembrandt House** - *Jodenbreestraat 4-6, 624-9486*
Open: mon-sat 10-17; sun 13-17. ƒ7.50. Trams 9, 14. (Map area E6)

**Amsterdam Historical Museum** - *Kalverstraat 92, 523-1822*
Open: mon-fri 10-17; sat/sun 11-17. ƒ9; 16 and under ƒ4.50. Trams 1, 2, 5, 11. (Map area D5)

**Jewish Historical Museum** - *J. Daniël Meyerplein 2-4, 626-9945,*
*http://www.jhm.nl*
Open: daily 11-17. ƒ8; students ƒ4. Trams 9, 14, 20. (Map area E6)

**Portuguese Synagogue** - *Mr. Visserplein 3, 624-5351*
Open: sun-fri 10-16. ƒ7.50. Trams 9, 14, 20. (Map area E6)

**WW2 Resistance Museum (Verzetsmuseum)** - *Plantage Kerklaan 61, 620-2535*
Open: tues-fri 10-17; sat/sun 12-17. ƒ8. Trams 4, 12, 25. (Map area F6)

**Hidden Church (Amstelkring)** - *Oudezijds Voorburgwal 40, 624-6604*
Open: mon-sat 10-17; sun 13-17. ƒ7.50; students ƒ6. (Map area E4)

**Botanical Gardens (Hortus Botanicus)** - *Plantage Middenlaan 2A, 625-8411*
Open: mon-fri 9-17; sat/sun 11-17 (Oct-Apr they close at 16). ƒ7.50. Trams 7, 9, 14. (Map area F6)

**Maritime Museum (Scheepvaartmuseum)** - *Kattenburgerplein 1, 523-2222*
*http://www.generali.nl/scheepvaartmuseum*
Open: tues-sun 10-17; in summer, mon 10-17. ƒ14.50; 17 and under ƒ8. Buses 22, 32. (Map area F5)

**New Metropolis (Science Centre)** - *Oosterdok 2*
*http://www.newmet.nl*
Open: daily 10-18. ƒ24 (after 16:00, ƒ14). Bus 22. (Map area F5)

**Kröller-Müller Museum** - *Hoge Veluwe National Park, 031-859-1041 / 031-859-1241*
This museum is located in the middle of a huge park in the middle of Holland. It has a big, incredibly trippy sculpture garden and a fantastic collection of Van Gogh's. Free use of bikes on site. Should be experienced. The park is open during daylight hours; the museum: tues-sun 10-17. Admission to the park and the museum is ƒ14 (to the park alone - ƒ7); and parking costs ƒ8.50. A package deal including return train and bus fare from Central Station and museum admission costs ƒ48.75. Ask for details at Central Station or the VVV.

# MUSIC

Many guidebooks say that Amsterdam doesn't have a "world class" music scene, unlike some of its neighbouring capital cities. What a load of shit, but that shouldn't come as a surprise with a yuppie phrase like "world class". In fact, even if you're only here for a couple of days you should be able to find all kinds of music. From community-run squats and old churches to dance halls and large clubs, this city is full of great venues and great musicians.

## HOW TO FIND OUT WHO'S PLAYING

**A.U.B.** - *Leidseplein 26, 0900-0191 (75 ripoff cents per minute)*
*http://www.aub.nl*

The Amsterdams Uitburo (AUB) is the place to start a search into who's playing in town. They have listings of all the music happening in and around the city. Look on the counter for their free flyer *Pop & Jazz Uitlijst*. It's updated every other Friday, and right now it's the best listing of bands and venues in town. There are also racks full of flyers and info about theatre and film. You can buy advance tickets here, in person or by phone, but there's a ƒ2.50 service charge on each ticket. Open: daily 10-18 (thurs 'til 21). (Map area C7)

### Shark
*http://www.xs4all.nl/~pipf*

Copies of this popular fanzine can be found at cool shops and bars. It's free and has a select listing of music being played around the city, as well as short articles, horoscopes, queer info, and other fun stuff.

### Way-Out: Alternative Uitlijst

I don't know who publishes this one page flyer, but I'm glad they do. It includes music listings for squat clubs and alternative movie theatres. Look for it in bars and in restaurants like Zaal 100 (see Restaurants, Food chapter).

### Irie Reggae Web Site
*http://cardit.et.tudelft.nl/~linden/irie/reggae.html*

If you're into reggae, look up this comprehensive listing of reggae bands and sound systems playing around Holland.

### Post Office Web Site
*http://www.postkantoor.nl (click "Concertagenda")*

The main post office (see Practical Shit) sells concert tickets. Their Web site lists all the big concerts happening around Holland. Find out who's playing before you leave home; that way you won't miss getting those Spice Girls tickets.

# LIVE MUSIC / PARTY VENUES

**Paradiso** - *Weteringschans 6-8; 626-4521*
*http://www.paradiso.nl*

I wanted to go to this concert hall since I was 14 and bought the album *Link Wray Live at the Paradiso*. Now I go all the time! Located in a beautiful old church, this is an awesome place to see live music. There's a big dance floor with a balcony around it. Upstairs and in the basement, are smaller halls where different bands sometimes jam after the main event. This is also a great venue for parties and performance art. I've seen everything from balloons filled with joints dropping from the ceiling to a live sex performance piece. Musicians seem to love this place, and big name bands will often do gigs here if they're touring Europe. Tickets here and at the Melkweg (see below) almost always go on sale 3 weeks before the show, and range in price from about ƒ10 to ƒ30. In addition, they charge a membership fee of ƒ5, which buys you a card that's valid for one month. If you're going to a sold out show it's a good idea to buy your membership in advance to avoid a long line-up at the door. Located just a stone's throw from Leidseplein. (Map area C7)

**Melkweg (Milky Way)** - *Lijnbaansgracht 234, 624-1777*
*http://www.melkweg.nl*

The Melkweg is located in a big warehouse (which used to be a dairy), on a canal just off Leidseplein. Although it's not the cheapest venue in town, there's so much to do inside that you get your money's worth. Prices are about the same as the Paradiso and they also charge a membership fee of ƒ5. Most nights you'll find bands playing in the old hall, or in the new, bigger, "Max" (revoltingly named after its corporate sponsor, some crappy soft-drink). Also on the ground floor is a photo gallery, and a bar/restaurant. (Entry to the gallery is free via the restaurant entrance on Marnixstraat wed-sun, 14-20:00.) Unfortunately, the rest of the building is often closed now, but if it isn't, explore the upstairs and you'll find a video room that shows all different kinds of stuff from Annie Sprinkle and Sonic Youth to underground footage that you'd never find anywhere else. There is also live theatre, often in English, and a cinema (see Film chapter). Flyers listing Melkweg events are available by the front door of the club (even when it's closed). The box office is open mon-fri 13-17:00; sat/sun 16-18:00; and from 19:30 on every night that there's a show. (Map area C7)

**OCCII (Onafhankelijk Cultureel Centrum In It)** - *Amstelveenseweg 134, 671-7778*

This cool squat club has been open for more than 13 years. There's always something going on here: live music of all types, cabarets, readings, and other happenings. Their small hall has a bar, a nice-sized stage, and a dance floor. It has a divey, comfortable atmosphere. Back by the entrance, an old stairway leads to the Kasbah café (see Bars chapter) on the second floor. The music and crowds are diverse and fun. Admission is usually ƒ5-10. Look for posters advertising their events or wander by. The complex also houses a sauna (see Saunas, Hanging Out chapter). It's located at the far side of Vondelpark, across the street and to the left. They usually close for a while in the summer. Trams: 2, 6.

**Arena** - *'s-Gravesandestraat 51, 694-7444*
*http://www.hotelarena.nl*

They stopped booking bands here a couple of years ago which was a real shame - the 400 capacity hall is roomy and comfortable with space to dance and space to watch.

But they still have regular dance nights, with deejays spinning drum 'n' bass and trip-hop on one night and '70s disco on another. Guests staying here (see Hostels, Places to Sleep) get a discount. Personally, I'm hoping they'll bring back the bands. Trams 3, 6, 14. (Map area G8)

**Maloe Melo** - *Lijnbaansgracht 163, 420-4592*
*http://people.a2000.nl/rstam/mm_home/mm_home.html*

They call this place the "home of the blues", but you're just as likely to catch a band playing punk, country, or rock. There's live music here every night and no cover charge. Walk to the back of the bar and you'll find the entrance to another room where the stage is. Don't be shy to push your way up to the front where there's a bit more space. This is a good spot to check out local talent. And if the band is bad, you can wander next door and see what's happening at the Korsakoff (see Bars). The bar opens at 21:00; the music room at 22:30. Trams: 7, 10, 13, 14, 17. (Map area B5)

**Bimhuis** - *Oude Schans 73-77, 623-1361*
*http://www.bimhuis.nl*

This is where jazz lovers gather. Ticket prices average ƒ15-30 and some hot musicians have played here. Often, on Tuesdays, they host jam sessions, and admission is free. I find the actual hall a bit cold and sterile, but the bar is relaxed. Decide for yourself. Other spots around town with *free* live jazz include Casablanca (Zeedijk 26, 625-5685), Bourbon Street (Leidsekruisstraat 6, 623-3440), and Alto Jazz (Korte Leidsedwarsstraat 115, 626-3249). Concerts at Bimhuis happen thurs-sat at 21:00. Trams 9, 14. (Map area E5)

**The Last Waterhole** - *Oudezijds Armsteeg 12, 624-4814*

Tucked away in a little alley in the Red Light District, this old bar has seen more than its share of live music over the years. It's a rock-and-blues-jam-session, local group, Grateful-Dead-cover-band kind of place. It's comfortable, especially if you can snag the couch in the corner, and there are a couple of pool tables, too. Bands come on at 22:00 and there's no cover charge. Open: sun-thurs 13-2; fri/sat 13-4. (Map area B4)

**Winston Kingdom** - *Warmoesstraat 123-129, 623-1380*
*http://www.winston.nl*

There's all sorts of stuff happening here at this old hotel since they completed their renovations: bands, parties, poetry. It's a lively, fun spot in the Red Light District. There's usually a cover charge on the weekends for events like the popular trash-glam night, Club Vegas, which happens every Sunday. The entrance is just to the right of the hotel. Open: sun-thurs 20-3; fri/sat 20-4. (Map area D4)

**Volta** - *Houtmankade 336*

Lately, parties have been occuring more frequently at this west-side cultural centre. The building's not too big, which makes for a nice, intimate atmosphere, while the high ceilings give some breathing space on a crowded night. Recently there've been deejays spinning trip-hop, jungle, and raï, as well as hardcore punk nights, and reggae jams. Admission to Volta is usually ƒ5-10. (Map area B1)

**AMP** - *KNSM Laan 13, 418-1111*
*http://www.xs4all.nl/~ampmail/indexe.html*

A lot of musicians hang out at the bar in this rehearsal space. Sometimes - usually on weekends - there's live music. It's a good place to check out local talent, especially during their "battle of the bands". They also host parties - Goa trance, salsa, African, etc. If you find yourself way the fuck out here amidst all the condo developments on KNSM island, it's the coolest place to stop in and get a cup of tea or a beer, and maybe shoot a game of pool. Admission, when there's a band, is around ƒ5-10. Open: sun-thurs 12-1; fri/sat 12-3. From Central Station take bus 32, night bus 79 (ask the driver to let you off at Azartplein). (Map area I3)

## Plantage Doklaan - *Plantage Doklaan 8-12*

At various points in its history, this building has housed a church, a hospital, and a school. Then it sat empty for a long time before being rescued by a group of squatters. Now there are living spaces, artists' studios, a breakfast café, and bakery (see Food chapter). Every Friday starting at 15:00 they host The Outernet, an afternoon and evening of food, music and hanging out. From time to time they also have parties here and admission is usually about ƒ5-10. (Map area F6)

## Kalenderpanden - *Entrepotdok 98, 420-6645*

The future of this squat is uncertain because the mayor and his cronies would love to see this warehouse renovated and turned into luxury condos. But while the battle is being fought in the courts, lots of activities are taking place here. They have a weekly restaurant (see Food), video nights (see Film), art exhibitions, and parties and live music. Admission, when there is one, is always cheap and is often a fund-raiser for a good cause. There's some really interesting and underground stuff happeing here. Look in *Shark* or *The Way-Out: Alternative List* (see above) for listings. (Map area G6)

## Inrichting Alternative Dance Night - *Entrepotdok 98*

This squatted warehouse is the latest home for this bi-monthly gathering of goths, vampires and everyone else who likes to dress all in black when they go out dancing. The music ranges from industrial to guitar to noise, and the organizers go out of their way to create a genuinely gothic environment. Often there are live performances. In the past it's been held every second Saturday of the month. Look for flyers and posters. Admission is ƒ8.50. Open: 22-4:00. (Map area G6)

## Cave of Satyr - *Haarlemmerstraat 118*

Here's another one for Goths. This one is located in the basement of Du Lac (see Bars). It's been described as "a chill space for Goths", with a couple of little rooms away from the dancing where you can relax and have a conversation without screaming over the music. It happens once a month on the first Friday and admission is ƒ7.50. Open: 22-5:00. (Map area D3)

## The E.L.F. - *Vlaardingenlaan 11, 669-2539*
*http://www.elf.nl*

Here's something new and trippy. Last year the old Belgian embassy, which is southwest of the city centre, was squatted. The sliding glass doors, wall to wall carpeting and video surveilance are still there, but the new residents have been doing some work around the place. One flight up, at the end of the hall, is the Magic Kitchen, where volunteers cook up a big veggie meal every night (see Restaurants, Food chapter). On the top floor is a *chai* room that's open every night. It's a very chill scene, with low tables and lots of pillows. Trance music is the order of the day, with the occasional deejay throwing in some reggae. Tea is only 50 cents and snacks are available. Sometimes there are open mic nights here with poetry, music and performances. The rest of the top floor gets packed during the regular parties (again, mostly trance) that are held there. There's lots of other stuff going on in the building including lots of painting, glass blowing, cool bands rehearsing, and one of my favourite places - the ping-pong room. It's a bit far, so ride your bike or take tram 2 and get off at the first stop after the highway underpass. Warning: in case it's not obvious from my description, this is hippie central.

## King Shiloh Sound System - *Various Locations*
*http://www.ndirect.co.uk./~shashamani/shiloh/frmainshiloh.htm*

The organizers of this reggae sound system have been around for years, but lately they've gotten their shit together and are presenting dances on a more regular basis. Recent locations have been OCCII and the Arena (see above). Admission is usually ƒ5 or ƒ7.50. Check the Irie Web Site (see above) for more info. Stay Positive.

## Westergasfabriek - *Haarlemmerweg 8-10, 581-0425*
*http://www.westergasfabriek.nl*

This old factory complex consists of 15 industrial monuments and their surrounding grounds. The site hosts music and film festivals, parties, and performances. When its current renovations are completed it will continue to host all sorts of cultural events, as well as providing additional parkland for Amsterdam's west side. This is also the home of West Pacific (597-4458), a restaurant that has popular dance nights every weekend. (Map area A1)

## Akhnaton - *Nieuwezijds Kolk 25, 624-3396*
*http://www.akhnaton.nl*

Already well-known for their African and Latin American music nights, Akhnaton is now featuring hip-hop parties and the occasional jazz/funk jam. African and salsa nights tend to draw a more smartly-dressed crowd than I'm used to, and it's a bit of a pick-up scene, but the music is really good. Clit Club, a women only dance night that happens once or twice a year, has also taken place here. It's only a five minute walk from Central Station. Open most Friday and Saturday nights. Admission is usually about ƒ10. (Map area D4)

## ADM - Hornweg 4
*http://www.contrast.org/adm*

This huge building along the harbour west of Amsterdam was squatted a couple of years ago after being empty for 5 years. Their opening party featured performances by Bettie Serveert (who played a fantastic set of Velvet Underground covers), and The Ex. Every party I've been to here has been great. And because the owner of the building is an evil little fucker, the effort you make to get out here will be especially appreciated. If you're not up to the long bike ride, there's usually a shuttle bus that leaves from behind Central Station when they have a party. They also serve a vegetarian meal in their café every Wednesday, Friday and Sunday at 19:00. The cost is ƒ10. Call 411-0081 to reserve and for directions.

# DANCE CLUBS

If you're into dance clubs, raves and parties, refer back to Club Fashions in the Shopping chapter: those stores all have party information. Most clubs open at about 23:00 and close around 4-5:00. For online info try - *http://www.logiclounge.com/nightguide*

**Mazzo** - *Rozengracht 114, 216, 626-7500*
*http://www.xs4all.nl/~mazzo*

Relaxed and friendly. Open: daily. (Map area B4)

**Roxy** - *Singel 465, 620-0354*
*http://www.roxy.nl*

Trendy and cool. Dress code and membership. Wednesday night is gay. Every third Sunday 18-24:00 is Pussy Lounge (women only). (Map area D6)

**It** - *Amstelstraat 24, 625-0111*
*http://www.it.nl*

Trendy disco. Gay on Saturdays. Good window displays outside. Good people-watching inside. (Map area E6)

**De Trut** - *Bilderdijkstraat 156*

Gay (mixed). In a legalized squat. Admission is only ƒ2.50. Sunday nights only. Doors open at 23:00 and close at 23:30. (Map area A6)

**Time** - *Nieuwezijds Voorburgwal 163, 423-3792*

Near Dam Square. (Map area D5)

**Club Zoo** - *Oudezijds Voorburgwal 216, 421-8325*

Trendy after-hours club. (Map area E4)

**Club 114** - *Herengracht 114, 622-7685*

Located in an old canal house. (Map area C4)

**Escape** - *Rembrandtplein 11, 622-1111*
*http://www.escape.nl*

Popular, especially on Saturday. (Map area E6)

**Sinners in Heaven** - *Wagenstraat 5, 620-1375*
*http://www.pulse.nl/sinners*

I've never been here. (Map area E6)

**Trance Buddha** - *Oudezijds Voorburgwal 216, 422-8233*

I have nothing nice to say about this place. (Map area D5)

**Soul Kitchen** - *Amstelstraat 32, 620-2333*

Disco, soul, r&b. (Map area E6)

*D-Monica*

**Flux** - *Rijswijkstraat 7*
*http://www.xs4all.nl/~flux*

Regular underground parties held here.

**Dansen bij Jansen** - *Handboogstraat 11, 620-1779*

Students. (Map area D6)

**Odeon** - *Singel 460, 624-9711*

Lots of students. 3 floors. (Map area C6)

# STREET MUSIC

Take a walk around Amsterdam on any warm day (and some cold ones!) and you'll find street musicians everywhere. Popular areas for people to play include Dam Square, Leidseplein, Max Euweplein, and Vondelpark (which also has a big stage in the summer) and Central Station. If I stop and listen for awhile I always give a guilder or two, which I think is a pretty good deal for having someone liven up the streets and people of a city.

*Robin Nolan Trio jamming in Leidseplein.*

# RADIO

**Radio 100** - *98.3FM*
*http://www.desk.nl/~radio100*

This pirate radio station has been around since 1986, and it's the biggest independent radio station in Amsterdam. They broadcast a wide range of shows covering many subjects and all types of music. They play an outstanding selection of music from around the world. Their schedule is listed in *Shark* (see above).

**Radio de Vrije Keyser** - *96.2FM*
*http://www.xs4all.nl/~keyser*

Born out of the radical squat movement of the late-seventies, these old-timers on the pirate scene became famous for their diverse, sometimes crazy programming. They broadcast a mix of politics, squat news, and punk music every Tuesday from 11:00 to 20:00. Check out their excellent home page, which has an English section.

**Radio Patapoe** - *97.2FM*
*http://www.desk.nl/~ptp*

Power to the pirates. Diverse programming (when they're on the air), since 1989, featuring all kinds of cool music. All with no commercials. Yes!

**BAR FM** - *92.9FM*

Amsterdam's newest pirate radio station is off the air at the moment, but I believe it's just temporary.

**BBC World Service** - *648AM*
*http://www.BBC.co.uk/worldservice*

Various shows, but best of all news in English every hour on the hour (except a couple of times a day when it's in German).

**MVS** - *106.8FM / 103.8FM cable*
*http://www.dds.nl/~gaylinc/mvs.html*

This is a gay operated station. Music, news and interviews are broadcast in English on Sundays from 18:00 to 20:00.

# FESTIVALS

All year long there are festivals going on in and around Amsterdam. Most of the ones I've listed are free. For any without precise dates, check with the tourist office.

**Anti-Racism Demo** - *March 21 (or the closest Saturday), Amsterdam*

This enormous, annual event draws huge crowds to celebrate the international day of protest against racism. All kinds of people hit the streets for a day of singing, dancing, and chanting that culminates in a lively fair. Look for posters or call the organizers at 676-6710 for details.

**Queen's Day** - *April 30, everywhere in Holland*

The biggest and best party of the year happens on this day. Amsterdam becomes one big carnival, with music and dancing and gallivanting and carousing. The world's biggest flea market opens for business: almost anything can be bought or sold. And despite the ridiculous new rules and regulations imposed on us by Amterdam's mayor, "fart-face" Patijn, over the last couple of years, it's still unbelievably fun.

**Bevrijdingsdag** - *May 5, Dam Square, Amsterdam*

This one celebrates Holland's liberation from the Nazis at the end of WW2: something worth celebrating. If you're interested in seeing some of the country's bigger bands, check this out. It's always a fun party. Fuck Nazis!

**Ruigoord Festival** - *June 21, Ruigoord*
*http://www.ruigoord.nl*

Over twenty-five years ago this town just west of Amsterdam was squatted and turned into a very cool community of artists and free-thinkers. Now, due to a very sleazy harbour development (which is just an excuse to bury toxic waste!), most of the beautiful nature around the town has been bulldozed and the inhabitants are being evicted. There were great parties at Ruigoord all year round, but their famous and very trippy summer solstice bash was always one of the best. The parties of 1999 may be the last opportunities to savour some of the few remaining vibes of Ruigoord. For news and directions check their web site.

**Park Pop** - *late June, Zuiderpark, Den Haag*
*http://www.parkpop.nl*

This is the 19th anniversary of Europe's biggest free pop festival and thousands of people will be there. Every year sees an interesting line-up of performers playing all kinds of music, but You'll have to truck out to The Hague for this one. Call 0900-340-3505 (ƒ.75 a minute) for details.

**Kwakoe Festival** - *mid-July to mid-August, Bijlmerpark, Southeast Amsterdam*

With over half a million visitors, mostly of Surinamese, Antillian, and Ghanese origin, this is Holland's biggest multicultural festival. It takes place over 6 weekends every summer and admission is free. The biggest draw are the soccer games, but there's also lots of music, food and art. Call 697-8821 for details.

**African Music Festival** - *first weekend in August, DHC Stadion, Delft*

Here's another festival that's outside of Amsterdam. This incredible feast of African music gets better every year. Some of Africa's best and most famous stars play here, in a football field outside of Delft. Tickets are usually ƒ30. Camping isn't allowed, but trains run back to Amsterdam all night. Check with the VVV for the exact date.

**Gay Pride Parade** - *first weekend in August, Amsterdam*

If you're here at the beginning of August make sure to see this fun, extravagant, and somewhat risqué procession of queer-filled boats cruising along the canals. Later in the day there are usually street parties. Call COC (see Cafés) or the Gay & Lesbian Switchboard (see Phone Numbers) for information on the route.

*Gay pride boat parade.*

### Parade - *mid-August, Martin Luther King Park, Amsterdam, 033-465-4577*
*http://www.mobilearts.nl*

This old-style European carnival is produced by the same trippy people who did the Boulevard of Broken Dreams some years ago. As the sun goes down on the circle of tents, barkers and performers compete to draw you inside, where you'll witness strange, otherworldly spectacles that defy the imagination. It's really something special. Admission is free until about 18:00 and then it's about ƒ6. Once inside, most of the attractions also charge an admission fee, but it's fun just to hang out and people-watch, too.

### Uitmarkt - *end of August, Museumplein, Amsterdam*

To celebrate the beginning of the new cultural season, Amsterdam's streets overflow with theatre, dance, and live music. King Sunny Adé and Dick Dale have both played in recent years. All for free.

### Open Monument Day - *early September, throughout The Netherlands*

On Open Monument Day over 3000 historical monuments in Holland - homes, windmills, courtyards, churches - that usually aren't accessible to the public, open their doors. On this day you can pop into any building that flies a flag with a key on it. For more info call 627-7706.

### Cannabis Cup Awards - *third week of November, Amsterdam*
*http://www.hightimes.com*

*High Times* magazine has hosted this marijuana harvest festival eleven times, and it's getting bigger every year. Several days of cannabis-related events culminate in the actual awards given for the best strains of grass, seed companies, and coffeeshops. It's mainly an American affair. Most of the events cost money, though the Hemp Expo is free and definitely worth a visit.

### Highlife Cup - *mid-February, Amsterdam*
*http://www.highlife.nl*

This harvest festival is really a Dutch event, although a few years ago they opened it up to other European growers. *Highlife*, a Dutch cannabis culture magazine, organizes the awards and the big party where they're given away. Tickets for the one day event are about ƒ22.50. These guys are serious: De La Soul played one year, and Cypress Hill another! For more info call 073-549-8112.

# BARS

**Vrankrijk** - *Spuistraat 216*

Even if this long-established squat bar didn't have a sign, you'd have no trouble finding it thanks to the building's wild paint job. Go late if you want to be in a crowd. Buzz to get inside. There you'll find a high-ceilinged room covered with political posters. Despite all the punks hanging around, they play all kinds of music. Occasionally, there are bands, performances, and slide shows, usually to raise funds for an organization or a cause. Saturday nights there's dancing in the back room. The first Monday of the month is a women-only night, and the last Monday of the month is a queer night. The Vrankrijk is one of the cheapest bars in the city: beer - ƒ1.75, juice - ƒ1. Open: mon-fri 22-2; fri/sat 'til 3. (Map area D5)

**Café the Minds** - *Spuistraat 245, 623-6784*

This is a comfortably run-down bar with a lot of character. It's located not far from the Vrankrijk. They have a pool table (only ƒ1!), a good pinball machine (5 balls), and they play grunge, rock and metal. It's a fun place to hang out and have a drink while you decide where to go next. Open: daily 21-3. (Map area D5)

**De Vaaghuizen** - *Nieuwe Nieuwstraat 17, 420-1751*

I've seen several bars come and go at this location, but this one has definitely got it together. They call themselves the "before clubbing hangout" and deejays start playing every night at 21:00 - jazz and rare grooves, techno, breakbeats. The split level space offers a cosy chill-room upstairs, a bar, and a little poolroom down below. Occasionally a local band like The Electric Fans will play a gig there and then the place gets packed. It's a very cool little spot. Open: sun 14-1; mon-thurs 17-1; fri 17-3; sat 14-3. (Map area D4)

**Café Weber** - *Marnixstraat 397, 622-9910*

When you walk in here it looks like a nice, ordinary, Amsterdam "brown" café. But downstairs you'll find a cool basement room decked out with old couches, big armchairs, lots of candles and a little greenhouse. It's a great place to sit around with some friends, even if the beer is a bit overpriced. Its location close to Leidseplein is a plus. Open: sun-thurs 20-3; fri/sat 'til 4. (Map area B7)

**Lux** - *Marnixstraat 43, 422-1412*

Just a few doors down from Weber, and in the same style, is this funky place. Deejays play here several nights a week, spinning stuff from pop to new wave to drum and bass. Open: sun-thurs 20-3; fri/sat 'til 4. (Map area B7)

**Soundgarden** - *Marnixstraat 164-166, 620-2853*

The giant photos of Iggy and Henry in here set the tone for music that's played loud and grungy, much to the appreciation of the leather-clad dudes and chicks that hang here. Actually, a lot of different kinds of people drop in for a night of pool, darts and pinball. Also, the terrace over the canal out back is a great spot to smoke a joint and have a drink in the summer. Open: sun 15-1; mon-fri 13-1; sat 15-3. (Map area B5)

### Brouwerij 't IJ - *Funenkade 7, 622-8325*

For those of you who are in town for only a short time, here's your chance to do two tourist essentials at once: drink a Dutch beer other than Heineken and see a windmill. The brewery in this beautiful, old mill sells its draft (with alcohol content up to 9 percent!) to an appreciative crowd of regulars in its smoky, noisy pub. On sunny days the terrace is packed, but it's nicer around the corner along the canal. It's a bit out of the centre, not far from the Dappermarkt (see Markets, Shopping chapter) and the Tropenmuseum (see Museums chapter). Open: wed-sun 15-20. (Map area H6)

### De Hoogte - *Nieuwe Hoogstraat 2a, 626-0604*

For my dough, this is the best bar along this strip. It's one of the cheapest, too: beer starts at ƒ2.25. The good music and relaxed atmosphere draw in a cool crowd of all ages. From the window there's a view of the incessant, frenzied bike and pedestrian traffic on the street. It's right next door to The Headshop (see Misc, Shopping chapter). Open: mon-thurs 10-1; fri/sat 10-3; sun 12-1. (Map area E5)

### Korsakoff - *Lijnbaansgracht 161, 625-7874*

This club used to be famous for its hard-core nights. Now its deejays and sound system play a mix of music: hip-hop, industrial, sometimes punk or a tune by Prince. The decor is interesting and the artwork changes often - check out the cool paintings by Mike Lavelle. Upstairs, where there've been techno beats happening lately, there's another bar and a pool table. Some nights it's really fun, with a lively, dancing crowd; other nights... dead. Buzz to get in. Open: sun-thurs 22-2; fri/sat 'til 3. (Map area B4)

### Café Sas - *Marnixstraat 79, 420-4075*

Walk into this café/bar at the north end of the Marnixstraat and you can tell immediately that it's an artists' haunt. Paintings, sculptures and other artwork (produced by the regulars) create a cluttered, comfortable environment. Candles add to this relaxing atmosphere and in the back are a couch, some easy chairs and a canal view. During the day they serve cakes and sandwiches from ƒ3.50, and soup of the day for ƒ5. At night, food is available in the restaurant downstairs. On weekends they often have live music and then the place is packed. Open: sun-thurs 14-1; fri/sat 'til 3. (Map area B3)

### Getto - *Warmoesstraat 51, 421-5151*

This queer hangout is very different from the famous leather bars that share this strip of the Red Light District. It's a restaurant and bar that's decked out in an arty, comfortable style and it draws a fashionable, mixed crowd. Tuesday nights from 17:00 is the popular women-only club, Getto Girls. And Thursday night bingo gets pretty crowded, too. Getto is open: tues 19-01; wed-sat 16-01; sun 13-24. (Map area E4)

### De Buurvrouw - *St Pieterpoortsteeg 29, 625-9654*

Occasionally, you'll find live music here, but mainly it's just a cool spot to hang out, listen to some music and have a drink. I like the fact that it's in a little alley. It makes it a bit difficult to find and that, along with the slightly twisted artwork, lends it an underground feel. If you like to dance, go on Sunday, when deejays play. And be careful when you leave - there's a dark stretch of canal around the corner on Oudezijds Voorburgwal where a few muggings have taken place. Open: sun-thurs 20-3; fri/sat 21-4. (Map area D5)

**De Diepte** - *St Pieterpoortsteeg 3-5*

Just down the way from De Buurvrouw, on the same little alley, look for the sign with the devil and you'll find De Diepte. It's a late night bar that gets packed in the early hours. Sometimes live bands like The Bones play there, but mostly it's just a noisy crowd enjoying the music ("beat, garage, punk & roll-o-rama") and beer. (Map area D5)

**Kasbah** - *Amstelveenseweg 134 (1st floor), 671-7778*

This mellow squat bar is in the same beautiful building as OCCII (see Live Venues, Music chapter). Its one room is fixed up with plants and colourful old tables with candles on them. Artwork and posters hang from the ceiling and walls, and fanzines are scattered about. It's a good place to find info on performances and political events around Amsterdam. Drinks are cheap cheap CHEAP! A big glass of apple juice (my poison) is ƒ1. Bottled beer starts at ƒ1.75. Kasbah is open when they have an event downstairs at OCCII; on Friday evenings from 22:00 'til late; and on Sunday evenings for a cabaret.

**De Duivel (The Devil)** - *Reguliersdwarsstraat 87, 626-6184*
*http://www.xs4all.nl/~deduivel*

A cool place that plays hip-hop and rap on a regular basis. Sometimes there's live music on the weekends. Weeknights are mellower. Peace to all the tourists, cuz I got a lotta love. Open: sun-thurs 20-3; fri/sat 'til 4. (Map area D6)

**De Koe (The Cow)** - *Marnixstraat 381, 625-4482*

This café is divided into two sections. Upstairs is a roomy bar that serves snacks and sandwiches. On weekdays, it's a mellow place to go and hear some blues or hip-hop, and to escape from the crowds of nearby Leidseplein. Downstairs, after 18:00, they serve meals that start at ƒ13. Open: sun 15-1; mon-thurs 16-1; fri 16-3; sat 15-3. (Map area B7)

**Du Lac** - *Haarlemmerstraat 118, 624-4265*

This place has lots of little rooms and corners to sit in with large or small groups of friends. Their attempt at "zany" decor doesn't quite work, yet it's still a fun, lively place to have a drink. There's a garden in the back and sometimes they feature live music on Sunday afternoons. Open: sun-thurs 16-1; fri/sat 'til 3. (Map area D3)

**De Pits** - *Bosboom Toussaintstraat 60, 612-0362*

This bar looks like an ordinary Dutch drinking spot, with wood floors, a pinball machine, pool table and dartboards. But instead of traditional Dutch sing-alongs, they play punk and hardcore exclusively. The owners are friendly and will play requests. You should stop by if you want to know who's playing this sort of music around Amsterdam: there are usually flyers on the bar. Open: sun-thurs 15-1; fri/sat 'til 3. (Map area A6)

### Café de Chirurgijn - *Eerste Helmersstraat 207, 683-3457*

A flyer promising "cheap eats and jungle beats" caught my attention. It was an ad for Club Ganesh, which happens at this bar every Tuesday and Wednesday night. The eats turned out to be not so cheap, but the beats sounded pretty good. And I like bars that have couches, easy chairs and a deejay. Except for the stinky toilets, it's a funky little place. They also have trip-hop nights and it can get packed in here late in the evening. Open: sun-thurs 20-3; fri/sat 'til 4. (Map area B7)

### Disco-Bar Abraxas - *Nieuwezijds Voorburgwal 171, 428-5072*

Deejays play almost every night at this smoky basement spot. Depending on the night, you might catch some techno, some big beat, maybe some hip-hop. Lots of mosaics decorate the walls. It's a good place to start or end some late night roaming through the city. Open sun-thurs 20-3; fri/sat 'til 4. (Map area D5)

### Bar Mono - *Oudezijds Voorburgwal 2, 625-3630*

The best feature of this clean, comfortable bar is its summertime terrace beside the canal. Although Mono is right at the edge of the Red Light District, it doesn't have the seedy atmosphere of so many other bars in the area. Deejays play on Saturday nights. Open: sun-thurs 10-1; fri/sat 10-3. In winter they open at 17:00. (Map area E4)

### De Bierkoning (The Beer King) - *Paleisstraat 125, 625-2336*
*http://www.bierkoning.nl*

It's not a bar, but if you're into beer you'll love this shop which is located just a stone's throw from Dam Square. Wall to wall, ceiling to floor, beer awaits you in bottles of every shape and size. It's all neatly arranged by country, with an entire wall devoted to Belgian brews. If you're flying home from Amsterdam, some of the more exotic beers make great presents. Check out the special offers - free beer mugs with certain purchases, and 10 free beer coasters with every purchase (hey, free is free). The only beer I didn't see here was Duff. Open: mon-13-19; tues-fri 11-19 (thurs 'til 21); sat 11-18; sun 13-17. (Map area D5)

*Don't drink and drive.*

# FILM

The great thing about being a visitor to Amsterdam and seeing a movie is that the Dutch never dub films. They are always shown in their original language, with Dutch subtitles.

The bad thing about being a visitor to Amsterdam and seeing a movie is the stupid, fucking *"pauze"* in the middle of most films. Presumably this 15 minute break is a big money-maker for the theatres as everyone files out to buy beer, coffee, and junk food. What it really is though, is an abrupt, unwelcome interruption of the film that never fails to come at the worst moment. Don't say I didn't warn you.

The big first-run theatres are centred mostly around Leidseplein. The cheapest time to catch a flick at one of them is on Saturday and Sunday mornings when the price is only ƒ7.50. Otherwise they are expensive: ƒ12.50 (weekday matinees); ƒ15 (evenings and weekends). Some longer movies may cost even more, so always ask the price. Some of the more interesting, little, or alternative theatres are listed below.

For movie info pick up *De Week Agenda*, a free weekly listing of film and other events around Amsterdam. It's published every Thursday and is available in bars, restaurants and theatres. Each of the big commercial theatres also posts a schedule of all the current first-run screenings in Amsterdam near their main entrance. Online, you can find out what's playing at: *http://valley.interact.nl/av/film/FILMWEEK/sortbios.html*

# THEATRES

**Tuschinski** - *Reguliersbreestraat 26-28, 626-2633*

This Art Deco theatre opened in 1921 and it might just be the most beautiful movie theatre anywhere. Although it's expensive, it's worth the price to see a film in the main hall (theatre #1). Occasionally - usually on Sunday mornings - classic silent films are screened with live organ music: quite an impressive spectacle. Go early so you have time to look at the ornate lobby/café. This is where the queen goes to see movies. (Map area D6)

**Nederlands Film Museum** - *Vondelpark 3, 589-1400*
*http://www.dds.nl/~nfm/E_index.html*

This museum/cinema/café is situated in a big old mansion in Vondelpark. They screen a couple of different films every day in their two pretty theatres. The admission price is ƒ12,50 and there's no *pauze*. You can pick up a monthly listing in the lobby. It's in Dutch, but check where the film was made because they show many from the US (VS) and Britain (GB). Some foreign films have a little "eo" listed next to them, which stands for *engels ondertiteld* - English subtitles. The two small theatres here show everything from old b+w classics, to rock 'n roll films, to women-in-prison flicks. Weather permitting, every Saturday night in the summer, a big screen is set up outside and a movie is shown for free. The café is also very nice (see Vertigo, Café chapter). (Map area A8)

**Filmhuis Cavia** - *Van Hallstraat 52-1, 681-1419*

This little cinema lies just west of the city centre over a boxing club. It seats about 40 and its rep programme runs every Tuesday and Wednesday. Bottled beer in their café is only ƒ1.75 and admission is a very reasonable ƒ7. Films start at 21:00. Closed in summer. (Map area A2)

**Cinema de Balie** - *Kleine-Gartmanplantsoen 10, 553-5100*
*http:/www.balie.nl*

When they added film screenings to its other activities - café, theatre, digital city, and gallery - the Balie truly became a multimedia centre. They're showing very cool films every Friday, Saturday, and sometimes Sunday nights, and many of them are in English. De Balie is located just off Leidseplein. Admission is ƒ10. Films start at 23:00. (Map area C7)

**Kriterion** - *Roeterstraat 170, 625-1479*
*http://www.kriterion.nl*

There's always an interesting mix of first-run and classic films being shown on the two screens of this art-house theatre. It's located not too far from the Arena (see Hostels, Places to Sleep). They also have a relaxed, busy café in the lobby. The last time I saw a movie here, someone stole my bike from out front. Admission: sun-thurs ƒ12,50; fri/sat ƒ13,50. (Map area F7)

**Desmet** - *Plantage Middenlaan 4A, 627-3434*

This beautiful Art Deco theatre used to be a volunteer-supported, independent cinema, but it was recently swallowed up by the huge mainstream chain, Pathé. The Desmet's programming seems a little more staid now (they've cancelled their famous weekly gay film series), but at least the policy of not inflicting commercials or *pauzes* on their audiences has been maintained. And admission on Monday nights is only ƒ6 - one of the best film deals in town. The rest of the week tickets cost ƒ12.50 unless you find four people to go with you and buy a *"rittenkaart"* of five tickets for ƒ50. There's a café in the lobby. (Map area F6)

**Cinecentre** - *Lijnbaansgracht 236, 623-6615*

On Sundays mornings at 11:00 films are screened here for only ƒ7. The rest of the week they charge ƒ10 for matinees, and at night, ƒ13.50. There are several small theatres in here, most showing foreign films so make sure to ask if the subtitles are in English. The Cinecentre is right across from the Melkweg (see Music chapter). (Map area C7)

**de Uitkijk** - *Prinsengracht 452, 623-7460*
*http://www.uitkijk.nl*

They show arty first-run stuff here that most of the big theatres ignore, and there's no *pauze*. Located right by Leidsestraat and Gary's Muffins (see Cafés). Admission: mon-thurs ƒ13; fri-sun ƒ14. (Map area C7)

**Melkweg Cinema** - *Lijnbaansgracht 234-A, 624-1777*
*http://www.melkweg.nl*

Upstairs at the Melkweg (see Live Venues, Music chapter), there's a cinema that shows interesting retrospectives (for instance, films by Cronenberg, classic porn, or martial arts). There is no *pauze*. Admission is ƒ7.50 plus ƒ5 for a one-month membership; their weekend midnight screenings are ƒ10. After the movie you're free to wander around if the club is open. (Map area C7)

**Rialto** - *Ceintuurbaan 338, 675-3994*
*http://www.xs4all.nl/~rialto*

The Rialto is an independent theatre with two screens. They show some interesting films, but they're mostly foreign, so remember to call to check the language of the subtitles. Admission is ƒ12.50 through the week and ƒ15 on weekends, but cheaper during the day. This is also the home of Moviezone (*http://www.moviezone.nl*). If you're 25 or under, you can attend their weekly screenings for only ƒ7. These films are screened every Friday at 15:30 and they show some pretty good stuff. "Grown-ups" pay full price.

**Soeterijn** - *Linneausstraat 2, 568-8252*

This theatre, attached to the Tropenmuseum, shows rarely-screened films from all around the world. They're often presented in a series - a month of comedies from Iran, for example. Call to find out if the subtitles are in English (they usually are). Admission: ƒ12.50. (Map area H7)

**De Kalenderpanden** - *Entrepotdok 98, 420-6645*

Also known as Entrepotdok (see Live music/Party venues, Music Chapter), videos are shown here most Thursday nights at 21:00. It's in an old, squatted warehouse, so don't expect luxury seating, but they do have a giant screen, a cheap bar, and the price is very affordable: free! For listings pick up a copy of the *Way-out Alternative Lijst* (see Music). (Map area G6)

**The Movies** - *Haarlemmerdijk 161, 638-6016*
*http://www.themovies.nl*

There's usually at least one second-run US or British film playing in one of the four small halls that make up this theatre. But the admission ain't cheap (ƒ13.50-ƒ15). This is the oldest cinema still in use in Amsterdam and its little lobby is beautiful. (Map area C2)

**The City** - *Leidseplein, 623-4570*

Totally mainstream, but the giant screen and excellent sound system in theatre #1 are great for movies like *Starship Troopers*. No *pauze* here either. (Map area C7)

# FILM FESTIVALS

**Bioscoop Dag (Cinema Day)** - *April; 679-9261*

Almost all the mainstream movie theatres in Holland drop their prices to ƒ5 on this day. Tickets go on sale three days in advance and the newer films always sell out. I usually see two or three movies on Bioscoop Dag, one of my favourite Dutch holidays.

**International Documentary Film Festival** - *early December*
*http://www.idfa.nl*

If you're in town at this time of year, look out for info on this famous festival. It's the biggest festival of its kind in the world, with over 2000 documentary films screened at several theatres around town. Visit their web site or call 626-1939 to find out more.

# MISCELLANEOUS FILM STUFF

### De Filmcorner - *Marnixstraat 263, 624-1974*

This little shop is packed with used videos and films at good prices. Most of it's porno, but they've also got weird shit like super-8 Bruce Lee films and Jerry Lewis movies dubbed into German! Open: mon-fri 9-12 and 13-17:30; sat 9-16. (Map area B4)

### The Silver Screen - *Haarlemmerdijk 94, 638-1341*

New and used books and magazines all about film. Lots of good stuff to browse through here, including posters, cards, videos, and laser discs. Other places to look for this kind of stuff are Cine-Qua-Non (Staalstraat 14, 625-5588) and, for posters, De Lach (1e Bloemdwarsstraat 14). The Silver Screen is open: daily 13-18. (Map area C2)

### Cult Videotheek - *Amstel 47, 622-7843*
*http://www.cultvideo.nl*

As a tourist, you probably won't end up here, but this is one of the coolest video stores in Amsterdam. They have an impressive selection of over 5000 videos including foreign films, sexploitation, cult and trash, anime, and a lot more. They even have *No Skin Off My Ass* by Bruce LaBruce. Occasionally, there are second-hand videos for sale. Down in the basement is a permanent Betty Page exhibition. Open: daily 13-22. (Map area E6)

### Anime
*http://www.forbidden-planet.org/Anime/Shopping/shopping.netherlands.txt*

If you're looking for anime, get yourself to a computer and check out the "Anime and Manga Shopping Guide to the Netherlands". It's an excellent source that includes a long listing of stores in Amsterdam.

# SEX

Sex and lots of it: it's a big part of tourism in Amsterdam. The Red Light District is always crowded and colourful, not to mention sleazy. It's located in the neighbour-hood just south-east of Central Station. You'll find streets and alleyways lined with sex shops, live sex theatres, and rows and rows of red lights illuminating the windows of Amsterdam's famous prostitutes. This area is pretty safe, but women on their own sometimes get has-sled and may want to tour this part of town during the day. Everyone should watch out for pickpockets.

There is also a smaller Red Light area around Spuistraat and the Singel Canal, near Central Station. And another, frequent-ed mainly by Dutch men, runs

*Penis fountain in the Red Light District.*

along Ruysdaelkade by Albert Cuypstraat. But while the Red Light Districts are con-centrated in these areas, several of the places I recommend are in other parts of the city.

If you're interested in finding out more about prostitution in Holland, stop in at the Prostitution Information Centre (see below), and pick up a copy of the *Pleasure Guide*. It's full of interesting and educational news, facts, and stories. It's only ƒ3.25 and it's in Dutch and English.

In case you were wondering, the services of a prostitute in the Red Light District start at ƒ50 for a blow-job and ƒ50 for a fuck. At that price you get about 15-20 minutes. The condom is included free of charge.

## SEX SHOPS

You'll find them every twenty metres in the Red Light District and you should definitely take a peek inside one. These places all carry roughly the same selection of sex toys, magazines and videos, ranging from really funny to seriously sexy to disgusting. Remember that videos play on different systems in different parts of the world. If you buy a video, make sure to ask if it will play on your VCR back home. The European system (except for France) is called PAL. North America uses NTSC. Also, most of the cheap stuff is of poor quality and you get what you pay for. For better quality I'd rec-ommend the following shop:

**Female and Partners** - *Spuistraat 100, 620-9152*
  *http://www.femaleandpartners.nl*
  This is the coolest and classiest sex shop in Amsterdam. It's women-run and offers an alternative to the very male-dominated sex industry. Inside you'll find a wide

range of vibrators, dildos and other sex articles. They're always expanding their selection of books and videos, and they also have some incredibly sexy clothes that you won't find elsewhere. The rubber and leather wear is particularly impressive! Everything in the shop is also available via their very efficient mail-order service. Stop in for info on fetish parties as well. Open: sun/mon 13-18; tues-sat 11-18. (Map area C5)

### Absolute Danny - *Oudezijds Achterburgwal 78, 421-0915*
*http://www.absolutedanny.com*

This shop is also woman-run and you can tell the difference from other shops as soon as you walk in. The atmosphere is relaxed and welcoming: single women and couples will feel comfortable shopping here. The owner, Danny, designs a lot of the clothes especially for the shop. She also stocks erotic literature and books about famous women like Mae West, Brigitte Bardot, and Betty Page. You'll find sex toys, videos, artwork, and best of all, penis-shaped pasta! It makes a great gift for that hard to shop for person. Danny is also co-owner of Demask (Zeedijk 64, 620-5603), the famous fetish-clothing shop. Absolute Danny is open: mon-fri 11-19; sat 11-18; sun 13-18. (Map area E5)

### Condomerie Het Gulden Vlies - *Warmoesstraat 141, 627-4174*
*http://www.condomerie.com*

The first condomerie in the world and what a selection! They also have an amusing display of condom boxes and wrappers. It's a very laid-back shop that makes the necessary task of buying and using condoms a lot of fun. Open: mon-sat 11-18. (Map area D4)

### Nolly's Sexboetiek - *Sarphatipark 99, 673-4757*

In the back of this shop I found a bunch of dusty gay and straight super 8 and 8mm films from the '60s and '70s for only about ƒ10. I don't have a projector, but this could be a real find for collectors and I thought you might be interested. Nolly also has a big selection of magazines, some that I didn't see in the Red Light District. Open: mon-fri 10-18; sat 10-17.

### Blue and White - *Ceintuurbaan 248, 610-1741*

This is another sex shop that, like Nolly's, is in the neighbourhood of the Albert Cuyp Market (see Markets, Shopping chapter). They've been open for 28 years! They have all the required stuff plus a bargain bin full of dildos, other toys, and discount videos. Open: mon-fri 9:30-18 (thurs 'til 21); sat 12-17.

### Miranda Sex Videotheek - *Ceintuurbaan 354, 470-8130*

This video store boasts that it stocks over 10,000 videos. Its two floors are loaded with more porno than you can shake a stick at. You'll find just about every kink and perversion you can imagine, and probably some that you can't. Open: daily 10-23.

### Alpha Blue - *Nieuwendijk 26, 627-1664*
*http://www.crusex.com*

I don't know, but I've been told, the cheapest condoms, here are sold. Apparently videos are cheaper here than in the Red Light District too, but I can't swear by it. They also have a big selection of gay magazines. You can spot this place by the life-size Betty Page cut-out in front. Open: daily 9-01. (Map area D3)

**NVSH** - *Blauburgwal 7-9, 622-6690*
*http://www.xs4all.nl/~nvshadam*

The window of this sex shop/information centre always looks so inviting that I wasn't prepared for the cold, clinical atmosphere inside. In fact, the only reason I'm mentioning this place is because of the theme evenings that some of you might enjoy: transvestite and transsexual evenings, exhibitionism nights, erotic massage for couples, and more. Call for times, prices and reservations. Doors close early and (I guess) the fun begins. Visitors to Amsterdam are welcome. Shop open: mon-fri 11-18; sat 12-17. (Map area D4)

**The Bronx** - *Kerkstraat 53-55, 623-1548*

This sex shop for gay men has an impressive collection of books, magazines and videos. There are also leather goods, sex toys and the biggest butt-plug I've ever seen! There's a cinema and in the back are some video cabins. If you get really worked up you can run across the street to "Thermos Night" (#58-60; 623-4936; opens at 23:00), where ƒ30 (ƒ20 if you're under 27) gets you saunas, films, bars, and lots of sweaty guys. Bronx is open: daily 12-24. (Map area C6)

## A Note About Prostitution

The decriminalisation of prostitution in Holland is one step in a long, slow process of public recognition and acceptance by the Dutch people of the commercial sale of sex in their midst. Under Dutch law prostitutes are regarded as victims and only pimps and organisers risk prosecution. However, as with the laws concerning soft drugs, these are not enforced. Because prostitution in the Netherlands has not been forced underground, it is one of the safest places in the world for sex-trade workers and their clients to do business.

In spite of this progressive legal climate however, sex-trade workers remain socially stigmatised and are still often exploited. Many of them lead a double life and this is one of the reasons they have such a strong aversion to being photographed. (Don't do it: you're asking for trouble.)

Prostitutes in the Netherlands are not required by law to undergo STD testing. This situation is strongly supported by the prostitutes union (The Red Thread) and members of the women's movement who work to ensure the human rights of sex-trade workers.

# PEEP SHOWS & LIVE SEX

There are several peep show places scattered around the Red Light District. I went into one and this is what I peeped. In a telephone booth sized room I put a guilder in a slot and a little window went up. Lo and behold there was a young couple fucking on a revolving platform about two feet from my face. It wasn't very passionate, but they were definitely doing it. One guilder gets you 30 seconds. Then I went into a little sit-down booth and for another guilder I got 100 seconds of a video peep show. There is a built-in control panel with channel changer and a choice of over 150 videos. Everything is there, including bestiality and brown showers. The verdict? Well, I found it kind of interesting in a weird sort of way. There were mostly men peeping, obviously, but there were also some couples looking around. If you're curious, you should go take a look: nobody knows you here anyway.

Erotic Palace - *Nieuwendijk 74 (recently renovated) (Map area EB)*
Peepshow - *Reguliersbreestraat 40 (recently renovated)* (Map area D6)
Sex Palace - *Oudezijds Achterburgwal 84* (Map area E5)
Sexyland - *St. Annendwarsstraat 4* (Map area E4)

In the name of research I also saw a few sex shows. At some you can bargain with the doorman, and the average admission price ends up being about ƒ20-25. Inside an appropriately sleazy little theatre, women will strip to loud disco music. Sometimes they get someone from the audience to participate by removing lingerie or inserting a vibrator. Then a couple will have sex. It's very mechanical and not very exciting, but it will satisfy your curiosity. At other shows (like Casa Rosso; Oudezijds Achterburgwal 106; 627-8954) you pay a set price of ƒ50 to sit in a clean, comfortable theatre and watch better-looking strippers and couples. Again, it's not really sexy, but the show was more entertaining. I especially liked one couple who did a choreographed routine to Mozart's Requiem. It was very dramatic and the woman wore lots of leather and had several piercings!

You can access Casa Rosso's live show on the internet at *http://www.casarosso.com* You have to pay of course, but there are a couple of free "previews".

# MISCELLANEOUS SEX STUFF

### Fetish Parties

Amsterdam is famous for it's fetish parties, where people can dance and socialize in an open manner, as well as enjoy the dungeons, darkrooms, and play areas provided. There's always a strict dress code, (leather, latex, etc). Admission is usually ƒ30-50 and often tickets can be purchased in advance. For a listing in English of all the parties around town, pick up a copy of *Fetish Lights* magazine (*http://www.fetishlights.com*), which is available for only ƒ2.50 at Female and Partners (see above).

### Prostitution Information Centre (PIC) - *Enge Kerksteeg 3, 420-7328*

The PIC offers advice and information about prostitution in the Netherlands to tourists, prostitutes, their clients, and anyone else who's interested. It's located in the heart of the Red Light District and is open to the public. Inside you'll find pamphlets, flyers, and books about all aspects of prostitution. The woman who runs the centre also gives a six week course in how to become a successful prostitute. The course (in Dutch, open to both sexes), covers topics such as history, health, and taxes. Closed Sunday and Thursday. Open: mon 15-19; tues/wed/fri/sat 11:30-19:30. (Map area E4)

**Same Place** - *Nassaukade 120 - 475-1981*
*http://www.sameplace.demon.nl*

There are lots of sex clubs in Amsterdam, but this one is unique because it bills itself as a "woman-friendly erotic dance café", and the cover charge isn't expensive. Everyone is welcome: singles, couples, dykes, fags, fetishists, exhibitionists, transsexuals, and anyone else. Entrance is *f*5 on weeknights and *f*10 on weekends. They have piercing and body-painting nights, kinky parties in their cellar (which has a dark-room and S/M corner), and special, women-only Sundays from 17-22. Open: sun/tues-thurs 22-3; fri/sat 22-4. (Map area B4)

**Amsterdam Call Girls** - *600-2354*
*http://www.Amsterdam-Callgirls.com*

This fully legal (registered at the chamber of commerce!) escort service is owned and co-operatively run by women. They've been in business for just over 7 years and have an excellent reputation. If you have the money (it's very expensive), and go in for this sort of thing, this is who you should be supporting: women who have taken control of their chosen profession and, as a result, are making their lives and those of their colleagues healthier and safer. Couples are also welcome to call.

# DICTIONARY

Note: "g" is pronounced like a low growl, like the noise you make when you try to scratch an itch at the back of your throat, like the ch in Chanukah. I'll use "gh" in my attempt at the phonetic spellings. Good luck (you'll need it).

**hello / goodbye** = dag (dagh)

**see ya** = tot ziens (tote zeens)

**thank you** = dank je wel / bedankt (dahnk ye vel / bidahnkt)

**you're welcome / please** = alsjeblieft (allsh-yuhbleeft)

**fuck off** = rot op

**do you speak english?** = spreekt uw engels? (spreykt oo angles)

**how much does that cost?** = hoe veel kost dat? (hoo feyl cost dat)

**free** = gratis (ghrah-tis)

**stoned as a shrimp** = stoned als een garnaal

**got a light?** = vuurtje? (foortchye)

**rolling paper** = vloeitje (flu-ee-chye)

**to smoke grass** = blow

**to blowjob** = pijpen (pie-pen)

**store** = winkel (veenkel)

**delicious** = lekker

**food, to eat, meal** = eten (ayten)

**rice / noodles** = nasi / bami (in Indonesian restaurants)

**bon apetit** = eet smakelijk (ate sma-ke-lik)

**dessert** = toetje (too-chye)

**cosy** = gezellig (ghezeligh)

**really?** = echt waar? (eght var)

**what a drag** = wat jammer (vhat yahmmer)

**juice** = sap

**cheers** = proost

**watch out** = pas op

**squat** = kraak (krahk)

**fag** = nicht (nickte)

**dykes** = potten

**bicycle** = fiets (feets)

**left** = links (leenks)

**right** = rechts

**asshole!** = klootzak! (literally "scrotum" or "ball-bag"; kloat-zak)

**I practice safe sex** = Ik vrij veilig (Ik fry file-igh)

# DICTIONARY (continued)

| | | |
|---|---|---|
| **1** | = | een (eyn) |
| **2** | = | twee (tvey) |
| **3** | = | drie (dree) |
| **4** | = | vier (feer) |
| **5** | = | vijf (fife) |
| **6** | = | zes (zes) |
| **7** | = | zeven (zeven) |
| **8** | = | acht (ahcht) |
| **9** | = | negen (nayghen) |
| **10** | = | tien (teen) |

**1 ounce** = 28 grams
**1 kilo** = 2.2 pounds

### Days:

| | | | |
|---|---|---|---|
| **mon** | = | ma | (maandag) |
| **tues** | = | di | (dinsdag) |
| **wed** | = | wo | (woensdag) |
| **thurs** | = | do | (donderdag) |
| **fri** | = | vri | (vrijdag) |
| **sat** | = | za | (zaterdag) |
| **sun** | = | zo | (zondag) |

### Temperatures:

| °F | | °C |
|---|---|---|
| 104 | = | 40 |
| 95 | = | 35 |
| 86 | = | 30 |
| 77 | = | 25 |
| 68 | = | 20 |
| 59 | = | 15 |
| 50 | = | 10 |
| 41 | = | 5 |
| 32 | = | 0 |
| 23 | = | -5 |
| 14 | = | -10 |
| 5 | = | -15 |
| -4 | = | -20 |
| -13 | = | -25 |

| | | |
|---|---|---|
| **cold** | = | koud (cowd) |
| **hot** | = | heet (hate) |
| **rain** | = | regen (ray-ghen) |

### Time:

| | |
|---|---|
| 12 noon | 12:00 |
| 1 pm | 13:00 |
| 2 pm | 14:00 |
| 3 pm | 15:00 |
| 4 pm | 16:00 |
| 5 pm | 17:00 |
| 6 pm | 18:00 |
| 7 pm | 19:00 |
| 8 pm | 20:00 |
| 9 pm | 21:00 |
| 10 pm | 22:00 |
| 11 pm | 23:00 |
| midnight | 00:00 |
| 1 am | 01:00 |
| 2 am | 02:00 |
| 3 am | 03:00 |
| etc.. | |

**what time is it?** = hoe
laat is het (who laht is het)

# PHONE NUMBERS

## EMERGENCY & HEALTH

**Emergency:** (police, ambulance, fire) 112

**Police:** (non-emergency) 559-9111

**First Aid:** (OLVG Hospital, 1st Oosterparkstraat 179) 599-9111

**Sexual Assault Help Line:** (mon-fri 10:30-23:30; sat-sun 15:30-23:30) 613-0245

**Crisis Help Line:** 675-7575

**Anti-Discrimination Office:** (complaints about fascism and racism; mon-fri 9-17) 638-5551

**Doctor Referral Service:** (24 hours; ƒ1/min) 0900-503-2042

**Health Clinic for the Uninsured:** (Gezondheidswinkel De Witte Jas, de Wittenstraat 43-45; mon 12-17, 19-20:30; tues/thurs 12-17; wed 19-20:30) 688-1140

**Women's Health Centre:** (free advice and referrals, but no in-house docs; Vrouwengezondheidscentrum Isis, Obiplein 14; mon-fri 10-13; thurs 19-22) 693-4358

**Travellers Vaccination Clinic:** (GG & GD, Nieuwe Achtergracht 100; mon-fri 8-10) 555-5370

**Dentist Referral Service:** (24 hours; ƒ.45/min) 0900-821-2230

**ACTA Dental Clinic:** (cheap treatment by students; mon-fri 8-17:30) 518-8888

**Pharmacies Info Line:** (includes after-hours locations; message is in Dutch) 694-8709

**Aids Info Line:** (anonymous consultation about aids and safe sex; mon-fri 14-22) 0800-022-2220

**STD Clinic:** (free and anonymous treatment; GG&GD, Groenburgwal 44; mon-fri 8-10:30, 13:30-15:30, or by appt.) 555-5822

**Birth Control Clinic:** (Aletta Jacobshuis, Overtoom 323; mon-fri 9-16:30; tues/thurs 19:15-21) 616-6222

**Abortion Clinics:** (MR'70) 624-5426; (Polikliniek Oosterpark) 693-215; (info line about these and other clinics; mon-fri 9-21; ƒ1/min; choose A2" to be connected to an advisor) 06 93 98

**Legal Aid Clinic:** (mon-thurs 9-12:30, 13:30-17; fri 9-12:30) 626-4477

# GENERAL INFO LINES

**Directory Assistance:** Holland (ƒ1.50/call, but free from pay phones) 0900-8008; International (ƒ1.05/min) 0900-8418

**Collect Calls:** 0800-0410

**AT&T International Access Code:** 06-022-1226

**VVV Tourist Info Line:** (ƒ1/min, which adds up quickly as they often leave you on hold for ages) 0900-400-4040

**Public Transport Info:** (info on trains, buses & trams throughout Holland; ƒ.75/min) 0900-9292

**International Train Info & Reservations:** (ƒ.50/min) 0900-9296

**Taxi:** 677-7777

**Schiphol Airport:** (general info) 601-9111; (regarding possible flight delays; ƒ1/min) 063-503-4050

**Lost and Found Offices:** (Amsterdam Police, Stephenstraat 18, near Amstel Station; mon-fri 9:30-15:30) 559-3005; (Public Transport Authority; 9-16:30) 551-4911; (Central Station) 557-8544

**Lost Credit Cards:** (all open 24 hours) Amex 504-8504; Mastercard/Eurocard 030-283-5555; Visa 660-0611; Diners 557-3407

**Gay and Lesbian Switchboard:** (info and advice; daily 10-22; text phone for the deaf 422-6565; http://www.dds.nl/~glswitch) 623-6565

**Youth Advice Centre:** (mon-fri 9-17) 624-2949

**Women's Centre:** (Vrouwenhuis Amsterdam, Nieuwe Herengracht 95; café open tues 17-23; wed/thurs 12-17; http://www.dds.nl/~womenctr) 625-2066

**Weather Forecast:** (recorded message in Dutch; ƒ1/min) 0900-8003

# EMBASSIES & CONSULATES

(070 = Den Haag)

| | |
|---|---|
| Amerika | 664-5661 / 070-310-9209 |
| Australia | 070-310-8200 |
| Austria | 383-1301 / 070-324-5470 |
| Belgium | 070-364-4910 |
| Britain | 676-4343 / 070-364-5800 |
| Canada | 070-311-1600 |
| Denmark | 682-9991 / 070-365-5830 |
| Egypt | 070-354-2000 |
| Finland | 070-346-9754 |
| France | 530-6969 / 070-312-5800 |
| Germany | 673-6245 / 070-342-0600 |
| Greece | 070-363-8700 |
| Hungary | 070-350-0404 |
| Indonesia | 070-310-8151 |
| India | 070-346-9771 |
| Ireland | 070-363-0993 |
| Israel | 070-376-0500 |
| Italy | 624-0043 / 070-346-9249 |
| Japan | 070-346-9544 |
| Luxembourg | 070-360-7516 |
| Morocco | 070-346-9617 |
| New Zealand/Aotearoa | 070-346-9324 |
| Norway | 624-2331 / 070-311-7611 |
| Poland | 070-360-2806 |
| Portugal | 070-363-0217 |
| Russia | 070-364-6473 |
| South Africa | 070-392-4501 |
| Spain | 620-3811 / 070-364-3814 |
| Surinam | 070-365-0844 |
| Sweden | 070-412-0200 |
| Switzerland | 664-4231 / 070-364-2831 |
| Thailand | 679-9916 / 070-345-9703 |